# MOORE'S LAW

## DANA BLANKENHORN

WORKBOOK PRESS LLC
187 E Warm Springs Rd,
Suite B285, Las Vegas, NV 89119, USA

Website: https://workbookpress.com/
Hotline: 1-888-818-4856
Email: admin@workbookpress.com

Ordering Information:
Quantity sales. Special discounts are available on quantity purchases by corporations, associations, and others.
For details, contact the publisher at the address above.

Library of Congress Control Number:
ISBN-13:            978-1-956876-69-7 (Paperback Version)
                    978-1-956876-70-3 (Digital Version)

REV. DATE:     25/04/2022

# LIVING WITH MOORE'S LAW: PAST, PRESENT, FUTURE

# BY DANA BLANKENHORN

# CONTENTS

# PREFACE
# IT BEGAN AT TOWER TV

Nothing has impacted my life, and yours, so much as Moore's Law.

It began as a magazine article by an aspiring entrepreneur.[1] In it, Gordon E. Moore explained how circuit densities on the new integrated circuits his company planned to build could double every year or two, for as far out as he could see.

He saw a long way. Microprocessors are now being made routinely with circuit lines just 7 nanometers apart. Within 5 years 2 nanometers will be possible. Quantum computing promises to take Moore's Law even further, beyond silicon.

Moore was a far-seeing man, but in my view, he didn't see far enough. The economics of Moore's Law have transformed every other area of computing, of business, and of society.

Moore's Law has created more jobs than anything since the automobile. Moore's Law has also destroyed more jobs than anyone ever imagined. It continues to do both. As an economic god it is Janus, two-faced.

I was born in January 1955.

This was 5 years before the integrated circuit was invented, in 1960. Gordon Moore published his famous article explaining Moore's Law in 1965. I was 10. My first experience with Moore's Law came at a college calculator store in 1975. I was 20. The same year two of my contemporaries, Steve Jobs and Bill Gates, founded Apple and Microsoft, respectively. In 2021 they are the two most valuable American companies, overshadowed only by Saudi Aramco, that state's oil monopoly.

But let's go back to the beginning.

---

1 Moore's original article is still available at the Intel Web site, https://newsroom.intel.com/wp-content/uploads/sites/11/2018/05/moores-law-electronics.pdf

At the time of my birth television was the future. In California Philip K. Dick was working up a story about a TV repair shop that would be published, after his death, as *Puttering About in a Small Land*.

He was writing about my father's life.[2]

Like Dick's hero, my father had a TV repair shop, in Massapequa, on Long Island. It was called Tower TV. From this humble storefront he earned enough to give our family of six a middle-class lifestyle, and a small home just a few blocks from the Great South Bay.

As early as age 3, I would walk a few hundred feet from my Presbyterian nursery school to his shop, and spend the afternoon waiting for a ride home. The store was maybe 30 feet wide and no more than 100 feet deep but to me it was a vast wonderland. I could turn a knob, and always find something worth watching.

At age 4 I was put in charge of filing schematic diagrams, hefty files that arrived by mail every month, in a box, from a company in Indiana called Howard W. Sam's. *Sam's Photofacts* [3]showed the inside of the latest TVs. It explained how they worked, and how to repair them.

The TVs themselves remained a mystery. When they were opened the air would be filled with dust, and a heady ozone-like smell. I could understand the TV's tubes, because I could see them light up. I could see how electrons would flow from their anodes to their cathodes, the current's properties transformed on the journey. But when I used a wire cutter to pop open smaller parts the schematics referred to, all I saw was dust. Still, I learned what the codes on some of them, like the resistors, meant. I could file them. I stocked tubes and resistors before I learned to read.

One summer day, when I was in elementary school and "working" in the shop for the summer (memorizing the daytime schedules of New York's 7 TV stations), a strange old man (probably 15 years younger than I am now) walked into Tower TV, holding a paper bag. Inside the

---

2 Dick's book is described on Wikipedia at https://en.wikipedia.org/wiki/Puttering_About_in_a_Small_Land
3 You can still see some of these old schematics at the SAMS Technical Publishing Web site https://www.samswebsite.com/

bag were what looked like metal bottle caps with hard plugs coming out of them. The man talked quietly to my father in a language I didn't understand. One of the bottle caps was "PNP Silicon." Another was "NPN Germanium."

I felt like I was in the presence of magic and did not know why. I know now. That bag the future.

Those things that looked like bottle caps were transistors.

Transistors were invented in 1947 but didn't go on sale until 1954. [4] They didn't conduct electricity, and they didn't resist it, either. They were semiconductors. When I was able to cut one open, it was dust, just as with the resistor. But this was a more magical dust. This dust could, somehow, do the work of the vacuum tubes I was filing on my father's shelves.

Vacuum tubes were the main point of failure on TVs. They were my father's source of profit. Vacuum tubes changed the properties of electricity moving through the vacuum. In the 1950s TVs had a lot of tubes and, because they were essentially incandescent light bulbs, they broke easily.

Thus, my dad's "free bench check."

People would bring TVs into Tower TV and place them on a bench that was always kept empty. Behind this counter stood my father, a tall handsome man with jet black hair and a mustache. In the shop, of course, I never called him "dad." He was "Fred."

Fred would open the TVs up with a nut driver while talking quietly to the customer. He would then turn on the TV and peer inside. Sometimes, he would tap at a tube with the plastic end of the screwdriver. This would cause the picture to jiggle, which would fascinate the customer and assure him Fred knew his business.

If people were "lucky," if Fred could tell they had very little money and it was clear a tube was broken, he would replace it, charging them just the retail price of the tube. They would write him a check, and he

4 San Jose State offers a detailed history of the transistor at https://www.sjsu.edu/faculty/watkins/transist.htm

would pull a pen from his pocket to help them. The pen had the store's address and phone number on it. "Keep it," he would say. It was brilliant marketing.

If the customers displeased him with their arrogance, or the problem wasn't a tube, he would scribble a repair ticket in his indecipherable handwriting, stick it on the top of the TV with some Scotch tape, then place the set on the floor behind him, still open, like a doctor checking a patient into a hospital. The shelves of the shop, and the floor, were filled with these opened TV sets. The backs and screws frequently got separated. There was a paint tray with extras, which in time was filled to the brim.

Tower TV was the first workplace where I felt comfortable. But the transistors in the man's little bag destroyed that life. That's because the transistors didn't break, which meant TVs didn't break, which meant that soon after I went off to Rice University in 1973, they no longer had tubes, either.

I don't know if my father understood this. I know is that he went off to California that year, my last spring in high school. He wrote back telling my mom to sell the shop and the house, to come out and join him. She piled us into a station wagon and dropped me off at college. When I came back five years later, Tower TV was gone, replaced by a real estate office.

The little bag began my life journey, of following perpetual and accelerating change. Down into the rabbit hole of that little bag, I knew as I stood before dad's former shop, all my generation's hopes and dreams would follow.

# Where We've Been, Where We're Going

In this book I divide the history of Moore's Law into three distinct eras.

1. **The Creative Era** -- Throughout the 20th century Moore's Law was mainly benign. The impact of Moore's Law was to both create wealth and improve productivity. Thanks largely to Moore's impact on computer hardware, everything from hard drives and CDs to fiber cables and radios, Moore's Law delivered the Internet and the dot-com boom.

2. **The Destructive Era** -- Starting after I wrote my first edition of this book, in 2002, the downside of Moore's Law became apparent. Moore's Law began destroying good jobs, first eliminating middle management, then financial intermediaries. Applied to software, Moore's Law created wealth around the world. Applied to content, it destroyed my livelihood. Its impact is now rolling through the music and video industries, and everywhere else, replacing intelligence with algorithms.

3. **The Necessary Era** -- This is the era we are now entering. Only accelerating change, made possible by Moore's Law, can save mankind from utter destruction at the hands of climate change. But that will only be possible if we adapt to the needs of the technology. We need to know what those needs are.

I turned 65 in the year 2020. My life with Moore's Law is ending. But the lives of my children, and your grandchildren, is just beginning. If you can understand where we've been, you can tell you where you're going. That's what this book tries to do.

I hope you enjoy it.

Dana Blankenhorn

April 2021

# Chapter 1

# What is Moore's Law?

*"The complexity for minimum component costs has increased at a rate of roughly a factor of two per year. Certainly, over the short term this rate can be expected to continue, if not to increase...That means by 1975, the number of components per integrated circuit for minimal cost will be 65,000.*

*I believe such a large circuit can be built on a single wafer."* [5]

Gordon Moore

*Electronics Magazine*

April 19, 1965

Moore's Law was written by an engineer, not a poet.

But seen in the light of history what Gordon Moore, then director of research for Fairchild Semiconductor, wrote was the most powerful statement of the 20th century's second half. It has proven as powerful as Einstein's $E=MC^2$ was for the first half of the century.

Moore meant it to describe only what he believed could occur with mass production of integrated circuits (ICs) his group at Fairchild proposed to make.

Here's how most of us understand it:

"Computer chips will get twice as powerful every year or two, with no increase in price."

Moore's Law moved electronic circuits from the periphery to the center of our lives and turned what we knew of conventional economics on its head, as thoroughly as Einstein overthrew Isaac Newton.

5 Electronics Magazine is where Moore's paper was published https://newsroom.intel.com/wp-content/uploads/sites/11/2018/05/moores-law-electronics.pdf

Moore's 1965 article even had an illustration predicting home computers. They would be sold in conventional department stores, although the picture is of a PC without a screen, sold to women (and their beleaguered husbands) alongside the cosmetics.

## Pre-Moore Productivity

Before Moore's Law there were two ways to increase the amount of work a man (or woman) could do each hour, their productivity.

You could get bigger machines or reorganize the work.

Thus, most futurists and science fiction writers in the early 20th century saw the future at scale. They saw bigger-and-bigger machines taking the place of smaller ones, requiring more-and-more management, organized from the top-down. They couldn't foresee that small machines might replace the managers, that intelligence might be modeled inside them. The office machines companies like IBM sold included calculators, typewriters, and punch-card machines for sorting data.

The other way to increase productivity, they thought, was through changing how people worked. This meant rigorously examining what was being done, mechanizing it as much as possible, turning the worker into the equivalent of a human robot. The great productivity hero of the early 20th century was the "time study man," using the principles of engineer Frederick W. Taylor and his *Principles of Scientific Management*. [6] Workshop floors were rigorously studied with an eye toward getting incremental improvements.

The assembly line reflects this ethos in action, and it was widely lampooned.

One of my parents' favorite musicals of the 1950s was *The Pajama Game*, centered on the struggles of a manager trying to fulfill the work of a time-study man. In the song "Think of the Time I'll Save," the time-study man muses on the efficiency of digging his own grave before he

6 Fordham still offers the original Taylor work at https://sourcebooks.fordham.edu/mod/1911taylor.asp

dies.

Another example is the "conveyor belt scene" in Charlie Chaplin's 1936 film *Modern Times*, in which the Little Tramp becomes so robotic at his work that he falls into the machinery.

Most views of modern life in the machine age seemed to involve some form of dehumanization, as with the 1927 German film *Metropolis* [7], in which workers revolt against their machine overlords, or the 1960 Billy Wilder film *The Apartment* [8], in which office jobs are the factory floor and managers abandon morality out of boredom.

Moore's Law stood all this on its head. Instead of making machines bigger, instead of making work more routine, automation would make machines smaller and make what intellectual work remained more engrossing and fulfilling.

Moore's Law meant that computers could become faster-and-faster, cheaper-and-cheaper, and could thus go into more-and more places. The only limit was imagination. Imagination, from high-quality minds, would become the gating factor to growth.

Moore's Law did for minds what James Watt's steam engine did for muscles two centuries before. By processing information as factories had processed cotton, but in a form that could be placed anywhere, the microprocessor made it possible to put an unlimited amount of intelligence anywhere.

## How Fast, How Cheap?

The same year Moore was working on his famous article, 1964, IBM was announcing its first "family" of computers, the S/360 series.

---

7 Wikipedia has an article on Metropolis at https://en.wikipedia.org/wiki/Metropolis_(1927_film)

8 After *The Apartment* was released co-star Fred MacMurray, by then a TV actor known for *My Three Sons*, was at Disneyland with his family when he was accosted by a woman angry at his portrayal. He never played a villain again https://en.wikipedia.org/wiki/The_Apartment.

The S/360 was built with transistors. Integrated circuits had been invented just a few years before and were not yet being produced in quantity.

The smallest of these new computers was the size of a few refrigerators laid end-to-end. Some models weren't delivered until 1968, and the project eventually cost $5 billion.

But all the new machines had the same Operating System (OS). They were thus "compatible" with one another. A program written for one 360 would run on all 360s. Eventually the S/360 became a big success, the first general purpose "mainframe" computer. The 360 also set a standard for all computers that came after – compatible hardware, and standard software. [9]

By the standards of the early 21$^{st}$ century, the performance of the S/360 was a joke. As designer Gene Amdahl, who later helped develop a "plug compatible" set of computers with his name on them, said, the S/360 would read an amazing 5 million characters per second! By the mid-1980s, thanks to Moore's Law, IBM was delivering faster machines that fit on a desk. The same power was available on a laptop just a few years later. In 2019, such performance is completely obsolete, even in a single thumbnail-sized chip.

This is the magic of Moore's Law.

When you double 1 and get 2 that's not a big deal. Even doubling 32 gets you to just 64. But when you start doubling numbers like, 32 million or 32 billion, you're getting quantum leaps in performance, and at the same pace as before.

That's the practical result of applying Moore's Law for over 40 years.

---

9 The S/360 was so late it cost Dick Watson, brother of CEO Tom Watson Jr. and son of founder Thomas Watson Sr., his career. Learn more on Wikipedia at https://en.wikipedia.org/wiki/IBM_System/360

# Moore's Multiple Dimensions

When I wrote my first version of this book in 2002 and even when I wrote a second, e-book version in 2010, I described the progress of technology through the eyes of the PC I was writing it on.

In 2021, the PC's future is threatened. In many homes it's a niche product, and it's no longer the chief profit engine of the computer industry. By 2030 it may be on the technology trash heap alongside the VCR and the floppy disk.

The PC's death illustrates what I believe is the key point about Moore's Law, its multi-dimensionality. Each improvement in processor speed spins-out into other types of innovation. This innovation can quickly make older products or ways of doing business obsolete.

The iPhone, barely two years old in 2010, was a "handheld Internet device," not a phone. It replaced the PC mouse, invented in 1964 by Doug Engelbart [10], with a touchscreen. It replaced the spinning hard disk drive, first delivered by IBM in 1957 [11]. with memory chips. It replaced the complex process of loading applications with a single click on an intuitive "app." The same device also did the work of dozens of older discrete devices, from cameras to filing systems to TVs and radios.

The 2017 model of the iPhone, dubbed the X, had a processor faster than that in Apple's fastest MacBook Pro laptop [12]. Computers as I had described them for 40 years – TVs for output, typewriters and mice for input, magnetic disks for storage – were replaced within a decade by screens acting as both input and output.

Even in 2010, however, the apple to apple (or Apple to Apple) performance comparisons were startling.

---

10 Doug Engelbart was eulogized by Apple Insider https://appleinsider.com/articles/13/07/04/inventor-of-the-computer-mouse-dies-at-88
11 Learn more about the hard disk and its history at Wikipedia https://en.wikipedia.org/wiki/Hard_disk_drive
12 A magazine matched the MacBook Pro against the iPhone in 2017 and found the iPhone faster https://bgr.com/2017/09/14/iphone-x-vs-iphone-8-a11-bionic-benchmarks-macbook-pro/

The 1977 Apple II, offered 4,000 bytes of memory, running a Motorola 6502 chip running at 1 MHz (or 1 million instructions per second) for $1,298. This included a keyboard but did not include a monitor, without which you couldn't see what you were doing.

By 2010, iMacs were built into the same housing as their flat-screen monitors. For $1,199 you also got 2 billion bytes of memory, running an Intel Core Duo chip running at 2.66 GHz (or 2.66 billion instructions per second). There was also a 320 Gbyte hard drive and a media manipulation program called iLife. While the Apple II could help you calculate your taxes, the iMac could produce a big screen movie.

In 2019, even this machine was obsolete. For $1,099 Apple was offering a processor that ran as fast as 3.6 GHz, with a 1 terabyte hard drive or a 256 GByte chip drive. [13]

This book was written on a "desktop" Lenovo 300 [14] with an Intel iCore 5 chip running at 3.44 GHz (3.44 billion instructions per second), and a 500 GByte chip-based hard drive that cost $160, installed. The original machine, with a 1 Terabyte hard disk, cost $400.

This book was finished on a $150 Chromebook from Acer Electronics of Taiwan, the text automatically stored by Google on servers many miles away.

## THE LIMITS OF MOORE'S LAW

In its original conception, based on Gordon Moore's original article, Moore's Law has physical limits. We're approaching them. The latest chip-making equipment used by Taiwan Semiconductor can produce microprocessors whose circuit lines are just 7 nanometers apart. With each generation of chip-making equipment, the lines between circuits get closer together. Eventually they come together.

---

13 Apple still offers a compare page, but that 2019 model was obsolete by 2021. https://www.apple.com/mac/compare/

14 PCs still don't wear out. When I edited my 2019 draft in 2021, it was on the same machine. I'd gone through two keyboards in the meantime. https://www.cnet.com/products/lenovo-300s-08ihh-sff-core-i5-4460s-2-9-ghz-8-gb-1-tb/specs/

But long before they came together, the electricity in these circuit lines creates magnetic fields that interfere with nearby circuits and create heat.

Intel recognized this was unsustainable after introducing the Pentium 4 chip in the year 2000. The original version of this book was written on a desktop machine running one. [15] Heat made the chip unreliable. Intel finally made two big changes, introducing low-power designs that created less heat, and "multi-core" technology that divided the computing load into virtual computers on each chip. With multi-core designs, Intel could go from 2 virtual machines on a chip to 4 to 8 – just as with Moore's Law. The PC this book was written with had 4 cores.

Most analysts say Intel's compromises killed Moore's Law. I would argue it just moved progress into new directions.


## THE NEW PROGRESS

When the original version of this book was written in 2002, I used Microsoft Office on my own computer. The current version is written with Google Docs, and saved to Google's cloud.

When I first published this book in 2002, I sent the files to a publisher called Trafford [16] and ordered 50 copies to be printed. Today, Amazon's Kindle Direct Publishing can create copies from a computer file, then just distribute the digital file. Textbooks can be produced the same way, delivering more up-to-date information to students at lower cost, in one-tenth the time it took to deliver them in 2002.

This kind of exponential improvement is happening everywhere. TV shows can be produced on iPhones, radio shows in garages. That's just the start.

On the Internet, collaboration is global. I first saw this in 2005, doing some work for a start-up. I worked with programmers in India, and we

15  This history is described on Wikipedia at https://en.wikipedia.org/wiki/Pentium_4

16  In 2021, Trafford was still around https://www.trafford.com/.

scheduled regular online chats. One day a second window popped-up, some minutes before the regular call, and it was some time before I realized I was now chatting-up someone in Pakistan. Ooops.

## THE SILICON GRAPHICS STORY

In the 2010 version of this book, I described technology as having a new, natural evolution, a multi-step process, leading from the imagining of a solution to placing a tool to solve the problem into any PC as a standard part. Here's how I described it:

1. Imagine a process. It can be an existing process or a new one.

2. Define a solution to the problem.

3. Put that solution into a specialized hardware device, using computer chips.

4. Turn the box into a single board.

5. Turn the board into a single chip.

6. Make the chip part of a standard PC.

7. Make the solution a program that runs on a standard PC.

The story of Silicon Graphics Inc. illustrates how this had already become, like the Roman God Janus, a two-headed monster.

The same forces that make rapid change possible also destroy the change agents.

Silicon Graphics was founded in 1982 by Jim Clark to build specialized computers capable of handling 3-D models. Its software was expressed in a "graphics engine," built into a series of very-fast computers created with the then-new RISC (Reduced Instruction

Set Computing) architecture, an improvement in older chip design independent of bringing their circuit lines together as in Moore's Law. (More on this in Chapter Four.)

In the 1990s SGI computers moved from the military-industrial complex to Hollywood. By 1996 some 20% of its revenue came from the movie business and animation studios.

By the turn of the 21st century, however, this process of building solutions into single-purpose machines broke down. By 2001 SGI stock, once worth $30 per share, was worth nearly nothing. On the high end of its line, it had pushed into supercomputing. On the low end of its line, it began supporting Microsoft Windows. In less than 20 years Moore's Law had turned its $10,000 workstation into a $200 software package. Silicon Graphics eventually declared bankruptcy and was sold for $25 million in 2009.[17]

The Silicon Graphics story is not unusual. What's remarkable about Silicon Graphics is that the company understood this from the beginning. It tried to get ahead of Moore's Law by creating more-difficult graphics problems and eventually supporting standard PC architectures. Its failure doesn't mean it didn't do great things or produce great products. The ability to solve problems simply outran its ability to come up with new problems to solve. It was ground down by the same process that birthed it.

Today, even the process through which Silicon Graphics developed is becoming obsolete. Solutions today are first defined as services, not as hardware. Applications are now "apps," designed from the start to run on wireless networks inside whatever hardware is available – security cameras, speakers, even watches.

## MAKE IT DIGITAL

There's another way to create progress with Moore's Law.

17 TechCrunch wrote about the Silicon Graphics bankruptcy in 2009. https:// techcrunch.com/2009/04/01/silicon-graphics-declares-bankruptcy-and-sold-for-25-million

Take an analog process and make it a digital one.

There are thousands of examples all around you, but the easiest one to understand is the one that started this book, your TV.

Philo Farnsworth [18]invented the first TV in the 1920s. It was, like radio, based on analog waves, Farnsworth used a long vacuum tube, called a Cathode Ray Tube (CRT), to create the picture by firing electronic particles toward a screen coated with phosphors. (Creating color meant using four sets of phosphors, for red, blue, green, and black.)

Even after all the other tubes in your set had been reduced to a single piece of silicon, TVs in the late 1990s still had that one tube, dominating the room, keeping the set heavy, and controlling the economics of TV manufacturing. This was the case when I was first thought of writing this book.

PC buyers were aware of this expense. It's why so many early PCs were sold without CRTs (called monitors when attached to PCs). It's also why many PC owners tried to re-use their old monitors as they upgraded their hardware.

In 1995 Sony of Japan introduced its first flat-panel TV display, which it called the "Plasmatron." I got my first flat panel desktop display in the year 2000. It cost $749, on sale. It helped edit the first edition of this book, but even as I was writing flat screens were becoming available starting at $350. Flat panel TVs were priced at around $1,700, down from $10,000 a few years earlier, Gradually, then faster-and-faster, CRTs ceased to exist.

Today flat panel displays are cheap enough to replace roadside billboards, and big enough to cover entire buildings, like the NASDAQ stock market's MarketSite building on Times Square. CRTs have disappeared completely.

When this book was first written thieves would rush to steal flat panel displays from homes. Now a 32-inch flat panel costs under $100. When the second edition of this book was written thieves were quick to

---

18 Learn more about Philo Farnsworth here. http://farnovision.com/chronicles/tfc-intro.html

grab iPhones from pockets and cars. As this was written unlocked cell phones were available at Amazon.Com starting at $60.

That's Moore's Law in action.

## MAKE IT MRELIABLE

As products with integrated circuits get faster, and cheaper, they can also get better and more reliable.

Computers were once defined by something called Mean Time Between Failure (MTBF).

The first computer, a tube-based system called ENIAC[19] was expected to break down completely within a year of its installation, and that with costly, weekly maintenance. The average computer chip, with billions of transistors on it, is usually thrown out when it becomes obsolete.

This is true for everything Moore's Law touches. Most computer failures can be blamed on software, not hardware.

As with the story of Silicon Graphics, this comes with side effects.

---

19 Learn more about ENIAC here https://en.wikipedia.org/wiki/ENIAC

# Chapter 2

# Meet Mr. Moore

As I rewrote this book, Gordon Moore was still with us, age 91, living in San Francisco.[20]

Gordon Moore didn't invent the integrated circuit, which took on the name microprocessor.

But he was there when it was invented.

His life illustrates a point I have often made to all who would listen, that the path to leadership leads through the skills of a journalist.

Seeing what's before you, understanding its implications, and explaining all of that simply and clearly, can make you a legend in any field.

Gordon Moore was born in San Francisco in 1929, then trained as a chemist at the University of California and at Cal Tech. After working briefly at Johns Hopkins University on the development of missiles for the Navy he met William Shockley, who would be the primary inventor of the silicon transistor. Shockley won the Nobel Prize in Physics for his work in 1956, along with Bell Lab colleagues John Bardeen and William Brattain. But it was Shockley's own work with silicon that proved most practical in the long run.

Shockley launched a new company to make silicon transistors in California and recruited Moore to join him. Shockley, however, proved difficult to work with, or to work for. When eight of his best engineers left to launch a new firm, backed by Fairchild Camera, Moore was one of the eight. Shockley dubbed them the Traitorous Eight [21].

The leader of the group was Robert Noyce.[22]

---

20      Wikipedia has an article about Moore that isn't subject to "link rot," its online location not being subject to change. https://en.wikipedia.org/wiki/Gordon_Moore

21      The Traitorous Eight is a great nickname. Learn more on Wikipedia https://en.wikipedia.org/wiki/Traitorous_eight

22      Noyce is considered the true father of Intel and was its first CEO. https://

Fairchild Semiconductor started off making silicon transistors, wafers of germanium sandwiched in silicon, encased in metal and with leads attached to the various layers. Some of the devices in that strange man's bag at Tower TV came from Fairchild. But the transistors had to be connected to one another, by hand, to create anything useful.

Noyce's Fairchild team looked for ways to connect transistors while they were being made. Their theory was that transistors could be combined in blocks of silicon.

In early 1959 another team, led by Jack Kilby[23] at Texas Instruments, announced just that discovery. Fairchild's contribution to the invention turned out to be its manufacturing method, created by team member Jean Hoerni [24].

## The Planar Process

The manufacturing system was called the "planar process."

It starts by burning or oxidizing a silicon block, at the same time diffusing the heat. Oxidation creates a smooth insulating layer on the surface of the block. This lets transistors and other components be drawn or etched on it.

It works because silicon itself is a resistor, resisting the passage of electrons, while silicon oxide is a conductor. By using the insulation created by oxidation, each circuit can thus be isolated from the others, and thus they don't have to be soldered together.

Circuits are created by etching them on the plane.

Fairchild filed a patent on its technique, while Texas Instruments filed a competing patent. Eventually, TI got the patent on its integrated

en.wikipedia.org/wiki/Robert_Noyce
23      Kilby lived long enough to be given the 2000 Nobel Prize in Physics. The prize is not given posthumously https://en.wikipedia.org/wiki/Jack_Kilby
24      The history of computing is filled with great, unknown stories like that of Hoerni. https://en.wikipedia.org/wiki/Jean_Hoerni

circuit technology while Fairchild won protection for its manufacturing process.

Kilby won half of the 2000 Nobel Prize in Physics [25] for this discovery. It's likely the prize would have been shared with Noyce of Fairchild had not Noyce passed away in 1990. Nobels aren't awarded posthumously.

## THE BIRTH OF INTEL

Moore didn't create the integrated circuit, but he was one of the Traitorous Eight. He understood it, he worked on it, and perhaps most important he knew how to explain it. He also fully understood what the invention implied.

Moore was still at Fairchild, as director of research and development, when *Electronics* magazine asked him to explain it all, a feature called "the experts look ahead." [26] His aim was to popularize the idea of the new semiconductors, or "chips" (the plane of silicon becoming a wafer that looked like a chip) in the larger industrial marketplace.

He succeeded. I'm a writer. Moore's article is good writing.

But behind the scenes there was trouble, trouble that would eventually make Moore into a billionaire.

The problem was that Fairchild was a camera company, based in Philadelphia, across the country from California. They made it plain they weren't going to name Noyce the parent firm's CEO. This meant Noyce would not have control of the money needed to build the team's integrated circuits. Noyce approached Moore about leaving Fairchild to launch a new venture, Moore accepted.

Their first name for the venture, Moore-Noyce, was (believe it or

25      Kilby's invention is described at the Nobel Prize site https://www.nobelprize.org/prizes/physics/2000/summary/
26      Most of the other experts in the feature are forgotten today. https://newsroom.intel.com/wp-content/uploads/sites/11/2018/05/moores-law-electronics.pdf

not) already trademarked by a hotel chain, so the two men settled on the name "Integrated Electronics," Intel for short. Based on a one-page business plan they raised $2.5 million through a San Francisco venture capital group led by Arthur Rock[27]. Rock had found the Traitorous Eight their landing pad at Fairchild and later backed Apple.

Intel's first product was a 64-bit static memory chip (SRAM). It could hold 64 discrete charges at a time, which could be designated 1s or 0s, in any combination. Each charge would be called a "bit." By using the American Standard Code for Information Interchange (ASCII), first created in 1963[28] to translate between computers and language in a standard way, the new Intel chip would hold 8 letters or numbers, each one called a "byte." (Half a bite, or 4 bits, was called a "nybble" but its spelling was finally changed to "nibble."[29] Engineers have senses of humor just like the rest of us.)

Late in 1969 Intel was approached by a Japanese company, Busicom [30], about making 12 separate chips for its new calculator. Intel engineer Ted Hoff [31], who had joined Intel the year before as "employee number 12," suggested the company could combine all 12 of the chips Busicom needed on one piece of silicon. Busicom funded the development.

Nine months later the chip was unveiled. It was 3 mm wide, 4 mm long, and contained 2,300 transistors. It had all the power of the ENIAC, developed during World War II to create artillery firing tables, which had filled an entire room. Intel bought back marketing rights to the chip for $60,000, Busicom went bankrupt, and the chip was released as the Intel 4004.

The microprocessor had been born.

---

27      Yes, Silicon Valley was built on a Rock. Arthur Rock https://en.wikipedia.org/wiki/Arthur_Rock

28      Learn more about ASCII at http://www.computinghistory.org.uk/det/5942/First-edition-of-the-ASCII-standard-was-published/

29      Nibbles and bytes don't mean as much as they once did. https://en.wikipedia.org/wiki/Nibble

30      Busicom is lost to history but it still lives at Wikipedia https://en.wikipedia.org/wiki/Busicom

31      Ted Hoff is forgotten. He shouldn't be https://en.wikipedia.org/wiki/Marcian_Hoff

Moore's article was part of a personal career transition, from the technology side of the business to the management side. He was executive vice president, under Noyce, at Intel's founding. He became president in 1975, then became chairman and CEO in 1979. He retired in 1987 and was named Intel's Chairman Emeritus in 1997.

In the early 21$^{st}$ century Moore, whose Gordon and Betty Moore Foundation [32] was launched in 2000 with an endowment worth over $1 billion, collected a host of honors, culminating in 2002 with the Presidential Medal of Freedom. Other honorees that day included the late baseball legend Hank Aaron, children's star Fred Rogers, and Nelson Mandela. [33]

## How Chips Are Made

Computer chips are difficult to make, but the technology is easy to explain.

It all goes back to Jean Hoerni's planar process. Silicon is a semiconductor; that is, it can be altered to either conduct or resist electricity. When you burn it, the resulting silicon oxide is a conductor. The planar process, then, requires that you simply draw the circuit you want, describing where you want the electricity to flow, then burn that design into the silicon.

This is easier said than done.

First, you need a very uniform piece of silicon. Second, you need a very precise circuit drawing, called a mask. Then you need to reduce that drawing from its original size to the size that can fit on the silicon, using ultraviolet light to create the circuit patterns on each layer of the chip. (Microprocessors may look flat, but they're very much three-dimensional objects.)

Along the way, chemical solvents are used to etch the chip and

---

32      Visit the Foundation and learn of their work at https://www.moore.org/
33      Here it is from the White House archives https://georgewbush-whitehouse.archives.gov/news/releases/2002/06/20020620-16.html

dissolve the coating around the etched circuits, called a photoresist. Next, chemical impurities called ions are implanted to change the way silicon in specific areas of the chip conducts electricity. The whole process is repeated, layer-by-layer, until the three-dimensional circuit is complete. To prevent contamination the air must be completely clean. Workers wear special "bunny suits" so they won't contaminate the space.

Over the years chip-making has evolved into the most complex, expensive, and precise manufacturing process in the history of the world. There are over 250 steps in the manufacturing process and hundreds of chips are made at a time on a large piece of silicon called a "wafer." As the process of making a specific chip is perfected, the percentage of the chips on each wafer that work goes up, and this improved "yield" drops the unit cost of making each chip.

The business of making equipment to make computer chips has become fiendishly complex itself, and very, very large. The leaders in the field of making computer chip-manufacturing equipment today, like Applied Materials and LAM Research [34], make dozens of different manufacturing devices.

## How Chips Work

The way in which chips work hasn't changed much since the Intel 4004 was released in 1970.

A single chip will include several different components, replicating the structures of a room-sized computer from the 1950s.

The primary components are:

A. The "address bus," which tells the chip where in the program it's working.

---

34    These were the market leaders in 2017 but things can change https://en.wikipedia.org/wiki/Semiconductor_equipment_sales_leaders_by_year#Ranking_for_year_2017

B. The "data bus," which moves information in and out of the chip.

C. A clock. With each "clock cycle" some data is processed and moved ahead through the program's work.

The chief way in which chips get faster is that chipmakers learn how to place more components on each piece of silicon or place those components closer together. The shorter the distance between components, the faster the chip can work.

When this book was originally written, in 2002 the most up-to-date chip-making equipment could deal with circuits as small as 50-100 nanometers. That's less than 1/10th of a micron, which itself is one one-millionth of a meter. By 2010, 45 nm and even 35 nm chips were being produced.

By 2018, Taiwan Semiconductor announced they could produce chips with 7 nm between circuit lines, while Intel was still at "only" 14 nm. In 2021 Intel expects to have perfected a 5 nm process. But this wasn't the only change that came about during the decade.

An idea called the "multi-core" processor, in which there are, in effect, multiple chips on each piece of silicon, first came to the market through IBM early in the 2000s. In 2021 Intel was producing chips with up to 8 cores each.[35]

One way to measure how fast microprocessors work is by how quickly they process information. The most common measurement for this when I wrote the first edition of this book was "clock speed." The Motorola 6502 chip that ran the Apple II had a "clock speed" of 1 MHz, or 1 million instructions per second. The fastest Intel chips of 2002 had clock speeds of about 2.4 GHz, or 2.4 billion instructions per second. In 2009 the fastest Intel chip in its line was the Corei7, with a rated speed of 2.93 GHz.

Multi-core designs complicate this. A chip with many cores may run at a lower clock speed than a single-core design, yet still process

---

35     Here is a full page on Intel's microprocessor chips as of 2021 https://www.intel.com/content/www/us/en/products/details/processors/core.html

more data.[36] The work on each core is done in parallel, so increasing the number of cores doesn't automatically double the chip's speed. [37]

There are other ways you can increase processing speed:

A. Instead of running 8 bits through the address bus at once, you can run 16, or 32, or 64. Each time you redesign the chip and increase the size of this "address space," you get a quantum increase in the chip's processing speed.

B. You can re-design the chip so that it breaks down complex instructions into simpler ones that run faster. This "Reduced Instruction Set Computing" was a very big deal in the 1980s but has become a standard feature.

C. You can put more memory on the chip, called "cache" memory, so the chip doesn't have to go off-chip for data. This is something Intel itself began doing in the 1990s.

D. You can combine a host of other functions on the basic chip, as Intel began doing in the first decade of the 2000s.

Some of these advances have the effect of making chips slightly bigger. When Intel switched from the 386-chip to the 486 design in the mid-1980s it produced key chains for the press, with actual (non-working) copies of both chips on it. (I still have mine.) The 486 was twice as big as the 386, in the way that the nail on your index finger is bigger than the one on your pinkie.

---

36      Here is a good explanation of that, from Create.pro https://create.pro/blog/cores-faster-cpu-clock-speed-explained/
37      Trusted Reviews has tested the latest Intel processors https://www.trustedreviews.com/best/best-intel-processor-3517396

## CHIPS AND MONEY

Before the integrated circuit, economists valued products based on their useful life.

Accounting for capital goods is always based on the expected "useful life" of the product, which also tells lenders the length of the loan needed to buy it. [38]

A car, for instance, is expected to last at least five years. When a business buys a car, it will "write-down" the value of that car over five years. Many cars, of course, last much longer. The average car is now 12 years old. [39]

Much of the equipment in a car factory is written-off over 10 years. Car makers also extend the usefulness of a single machine by having several car models made on the same "platform."

Buildings, either homes, offices, or factories, are expected to last even longer. You buy a 30-year mortgage for your home because the home is expected to last at least that long, not because you're expecting to stay in it that long.

Moore's Law has a different set of rules:

E. It takes time to learn how to correctly make each new chip design. The "yield," the percentage of chips on a wafer that work, starts very low during early production runs, and slowly increases. Thus, the cost of making a newly designed chip is much higher than the cost of making an older design.

F. Each new chip design is a quantum-leap ahead of previous chips in its performance, so the useful life of the design is short – no more

---

38      Here is how thy teach it at Duke University http://people.duke.edu/~brav/TEACHING/PS/PSCapbudg.html
39      Wolf Street tracks the average age of cars. https://wolfstreet.com/2018/08/21/average-age-of-cars-trucks-vehicles-by-household-income-vehicle-type/

than a few years.

G. All the factory equipment used to make a microchip is also replaced regularly, by equipment that represents a quantum leap in performance. The useful life of these machines is thus also just a few years.

H. Even if new designs aren't emerging, making existing chips obsolete, the yield is always rising, so the cost of a chip is always declining.

This lowering of costs (and prices), called deflation, exists everywhere, and in everything touched by the microchip. It's not that chips or equipment wear out, they just become obsolete as better and better equipment emerges, faster and faster.

Since products lose value as soon as they leave the factory the sales channel is also under constant pressure. The name "Apple" turned out to be an unwelcome pun because computers on store shelves do age more like fruit. They lose value as they sit on the shelf.

## The Magic of Deflation

The deflationary impact of Moore's Law has now been operating for a half-century.

I first became aware of this when I went to college. I had used a slide rule in high school, but the cool kids all had calculators. I wanted one. (Never mind that I was a political science major.)

The calculators I saw at Rice University in Houston, during the mid-70s, were extremely complex, and expensive. The most popular one with my classmates bore the logo of Texas Instruments. They were the home team. Hewlett-Packard also made good calculators, but they were a California company.

By the time I left college, the capabilities of common chips came to exceed the needs of even complex calculators. Prices plunged.

As PCs came into vogue, just as Moore had predicted they would a decade before, the need to own complex calculators also decreased. By the mid-1980s I was seeing calculators given-away as premiums for magazine subscriptions. By the 1990s even-smaller calculators, many of them with tiny solar panels on them instead of batteries, were being imprinted with corporate logos and given away at trade shows as "tchotchkes," or little gifts. (Tchotchkes were also called "booth candy.")

The power of chip-based deflation is undeniable. It hits different industries at different times. Engineers are always seeking new applications for microchips, more complex tasks that chips might handle. Once a job is found and a design is implemented, the job of making it better, cheaper, even trivial begins. Each new solution costs less than the one before and, since it's often based on fewer chips, it becomes more reliable as well.

I'll be discussing the impact of Moore's Law and microchip economics on many industries throughout this book. Here are the basics:

A. Each chip design is a whole lot better than the one before.

B. Yields increase over time, cutting unit costs.

C. Equipment becomes obsolete and worthless before it becomes unusable.

D. Deflation is constant in anything touched by the microchip.

# CHAPTER 3

# LIVING WITH MOORE'S LAW

## BEFORE THE BEGINNING

As I noted in the preface, I was raised by a TV repair shop.

Tower TV, in Massapequa, New York, on Long Island, generated enough cash to raise my whole family. It also helped other men raise their families, something of which my father was very proud. One of my favorite memories from growing up was watching Fred in his tiny office, built out of plywood in the back of the shop, hand-writing the paychecks of his workers.

In the 1950s and early 1960s TVs were a key consumer product. Production was always rising, but TVs were expensive and often broke down. They kept getting more expensive as their picture tubes got larger, and by the mid-1960s there were color models. For a brief time, my dad sold Admiral Color TVs, and one was eventually brought into the house.

As I mentioned before, fixing a set was often as simple as removing the back and looking for a blown tube. In addition to his "Free Bench Check," Fred also installed a "tube tester" at the front of his shop. I found this entertaining. People would come by with paper bags filled with tubes, inserting each in a labeled socket. The tester sat upright on the floor and looked like a pinball machine. If a tube failed the customer would proudly bring it to the counter, and I would sell them a new one at a "wholesale" price, even lower than they'd get with the Free Bench Check.

For the bigger sets I sometimes went out on service calls. This meant riding with one of my dad's employees in a panel truck, then lugging a large case up the client's walk. The bottom of the case held simple tools, including a soldering gun for repairing circuit boards. But most of the case held tubes, all arranged in numerical order, from the big 1B3 that had a metal cap on it to the 6SJ7 that was the size of a man's finger.

# THE TRANSISTOR MAN

When the man with the paper sack first came into my father's shop, dad's only concern was supplying parts for the increasing number of car radios he was seeing.

But the visitor had another message for him. He wouldn't have to stock as many of these new transistors as he had tubes. They were "solid-state," more reliable than tubes. You'll save money, the Transistor Man said.

The Transistor Man then cut open a transistor to show me. A tube was filled with tiny metal parts and wires. I could understand where the electricity was going inside the tube and had a vague idea of what it was doing there. A transistor was filled with what looked like powder. There was nothing inside to go wrong. There were no wires. About the only thing that might cause a transistor to break would be some trouble with one of its metal pins or an electrical short blowing out the whole circuit it was attached to.

The economics of solid state, and then of integrated circuits, would end the TV repair business within a decade of the Transistor Man's visit. Fred didn't talk about it, but I like to think he had a sixth sense about it, because he sold his business as I was graduating high school and drove himself to California. He was looking for work in the electronic security industry and emerged by the end of the decade owning a locksmith shop.

Tower TV was an early victim of Moore's Law. Today we'd say it was destroyed by automation. But Moore's Law would also transform the world for the better, changing how all things were made, and the way in which the economy worked.

# MOORE'S LAW ECONOMICS

Moore's Law stands manufacturing economics on its head.

In manufacturing economics, productivity comes from making bigger machines, or making slight improvements in production techniques. Progress is incremental, measured in a percentage or two each year. Inflation is a constant, because all production is based on raw materials and other manufacturers whose costs are also rising. This caps wages, which can't rise faster than productivity, lest inflation run out of control.

A "Warner Brothers" cartoon funded by the Sloan Foundation (created by General Motors' founding chairman) illustrated the process.

It was called *Heir Conditioned.*[40] It was one of three cartoons underwritten by the foundation of Alfred P. Sloan, who had been CEO of General Motors.

In the cartoon, Sylvester the Cat inherits a fortune and wants to spend it. Elmer Fudd patiently explains how mass production leads to mass consumption, investment leads to dividends, and this means a better life for everyone. The cat invests his fortune instead of saving it. The emphasis is on small gains adding up year-by-year. (Ironically the first cartoon in the series was called "By Word of Mouse.")

The economics of Moore's Law doesn't work that way.

By constantly creating new, faster computers, Moore's Law allows productivity to jump in great leaps. It's not just the chips themselves that make this happen. It's the uses to which the chips are put, and managers' ability to re-imagine how work can be done as a result. Computer intelligence is put in more-and-more places, and at each step of the process waste is reduced, as is the need for raw materials and labor.

Each new generation of computers has the capability to revolutionize entire industries. If the work someone does can be defined by software, thus done by the computer, the work will go into the computer. The economics of the industry will change radically. Such changes are tremendous, immediate, and highly disruptive.

In the 20th century each generation of computing changed other

---

40      Heir Conditioned is described at Wikipedia. https://en.wikipedia.org/wiki/Heir-Conditioned

industries. My business, writing, was revolutionized in the mid-1980s. Movie production was revolutionized by companies like Silicon Graphics in the 1990s.

And this was just the start.

## WAREHOUSES

Consider warehouses and a simple computer-based technology called the barcode.

When I was a kid warehouses were where businesses stored goods before they were sent to store shelves. My dad would often drive me to warehouses serving the TV repair industry, for parts he couldn't afford to stock.

For decades after World War II recessions were called "inventory corrections." Demand would slow, material would stay in warehouses, and slowly this word filtered back to factories, which would slow production. The time it took to slow down manufacturing in response to slower demand, then speed things back up again after the warehouses had emptied and demand returned, was the recession.

The rise of handheld computers with barcode readers, tied to computer networks, revolutionized this business starting in the early 1980s. They eliminated the time lag between slowing demand in stores and slowing production in factories by allowing stores to communicate directly with factories.

By the year 2000 employees at Walmart and Home Depot could carry terminals that scanned barcodes on the inventory. The counts acted as back-ups to computerized cash registers and networks that would communicate in turn with the chains' central computers. These in turn sent orders (and order cancellations) automatically to factories. Not only are the warehouses sending out just what they needed, but the factories could slow production too, within a day or week.

Stores like Best Buy, Toys R Us and Old Navy came to resemble warehouses and came to be known by business reporters like me as "category killers," driving out smaller competitors in small towns and suburbs. Downtowns were replaced by strip malls. It was much cheaper to build a set of warehouse stores by a freeway than to refurbish city centers or even suburban shopping malls. The biggest such stores, like Costco, BJ's Warehouse and Walmart's own Sam's Club chain were literally warehouses, with mass quantities of goods pulled directly off pallets, restocked by forklifts.

In 2020, even these "category killers" were dying, despite using the latest barcode technology. These are two-dimensional QC codes, which replace the lines with dots on something like a postage stamp. Amazon. Com is catching Walmart by taking orders directly from consumers, and shipping directly to doorsteps, at prices competitive with going to the mall. This productivity boost for shoppers has eliminated hundreds of thousands of retail jobs, thousands of stores, and entire shopping malls, which had become the suburbs' downtown.

This latest twist in Moore's Law Economics increased demand for warehouses. The difference is that while warehouses once were where bulk goods were stored for shipment, they're now where companies do what stores once did, "break bulk." The warehouses are run like retail floors, with orders coming in by computer and going out by truck. Breaking bulk at the warehouse reduces "shrinkage," theft of merchandise on the retail floor. It eliminates the need for salesmen, replacing them with "pickers" who collect merchandise from shelves. Over time, robots will replace the pickers, and retailing will be completely automated.

There's an irony here before moving on. The idea of breaking bulk close to customers is precisely what *Service Merchandise*[41] did before it went bankrupt in 2002. The differences are in delivery infrastructure, and the unlimited supply you get from networking warehouses together with computers.

International shipping was one of the first industries revolutionized by the bar code. Instead of packing materials on pallets into a boat, everything moved into same-sized containers. Containers are stacked on

41    I remember shopping at Service Merchandise. Do you? https://en.wikipedia.org/wiki/Service_Merchandise

ships, or on trains, with bar codes telling computers where they should go. A single "container ship" can move the equivalent of thousands of semi-trailers across oceans at a fraction of the truck's cost.

As a result of all these changes, the amount of net warehouse space used by businesses in the USA remained virtually the same between 1980 and 2010. Warehouses were turned to other uses. Some became rock clubs, others became rock-climbing clubs, and many older ones became residences.

Between 2010 and 2020, retailing also ceased being a middle-class pursuit centered on large department stores and became an upper-class pursuit shaped around high-end restaurants, with stores acting as showrooms for the brands that stocked them.

The biggest new market for warehousing is in the consumer market, the "self-storage" industry. Storage companies leave boxes at homes that consumers fill with their junk, then pick them up, combining bar-code technology with the process of containerized shipping.

These kinds of changes can hit all at once, but they don't hit all industries at the same time. Those who understand the changes first can win fortunes. Those who don't pay attention quickly go out of business.

What is called the "Retail Apocalypse" or "RetailMageddon" destroyed dozens of once thriving store chains in the last half of the decade. Toys R Us, Payless ShoeSource, and American Apparel, have all gone bankrupt Dozens of others like Sears, JC Penney, and J. Crew, were tottering on the edge as this was written. Some chains, like Kohl's, have adapted, renting out extra space to fitness centers and even Amazon.

But not all the impacts of Moore's Law act to cut costs.

Some raise costs.

# Moore's Second Law

A microchip fabrication plant, or "fab," is one of the most expensive buildings on Earth.

Not only is it expensive to build, but it's ferociously expensive to maintain. Each time a new generation of chips is to be made the plant's equipment (the most expensive part of the plant) must be replaced.

Each "fab" generation costs more than the last. Plant costs rise exponentially, not arithmetically.

I call this process of increasing fabrication costs "Moore's Second Law."

The plants used to build the earliest memory chips cost just a few millions of dollars to build, while today the cost is measured in tens of billions of dollars. As each new generation is put online, older plants become obsolete and worthless. It's ferociously capital-intensive.

It takes many billions of dollars to get into the chip business, and a return on that money must come very, very fast.

Semiconductor fabs are also environmental disaster areas. Acids, cyanide compounds, organic solvents, silicon tetrachloride and arsine gas are all produced by these plants. It was to avoid these costs, and to keep wage costs down, that many chip plants were quickly moved outside the U.S. By 2010 Intel had plants in dozens of countries around the world.

As this version of the book is written most of America's chips are being made either in Taiwan or Mainland China. While in Chengdu, China in mid-2009 – the last city west before heading into the Himalayas – I heard loud complaints about an IBM chip plant on the outskirts of town, and the pollution it was causing. China's lack of labor or environmental standards won it the business from an industry whose intrinsic costs were too high to care about either.

For the most part America's role in chip production today is limited to designing, organizing, and funding the industry. Hardware is now software. There are still some large American "fabs," like Micron Technologies' memory chip plant in Boise, Idaho. There are fabs in Texas, where environmental problems are often ignored, and wages are lower than elsewhere in the U.S. But these are exceptions. Even the production of chipmaking equipment has gone global – Applied Materials has plants in Israel, Japan, Korea, and England as well as the U.S.

Only in 2021 did the U.S. truly re-commit to American production of semiconductors. Intel announced it would build two new fabrication plants in Arizona, near where Taiwan Semiconductor had already committed to building one, and that it would act as a foundry for other companies' chips. [42]

Moore's Second Law has done a lot to make the world a smaller place. The costs of building and running plants to produce chips has brought employment, not just to the U.S., but to developed and developing nations around the world.

As Moore's Second Law has ground on in the 2010s the number of companies with the capital to produce general purpose microprocessors had been reduced to four – Intel, Samsung, Global Foundries (controlled by Arab money) and Taiwan Semiconductor. China was investing heavily in the business, however, and its willingness to subsidize such plants threatens to transform the industry in the next decade, moving even the intellectual property in chips to the Far East.

## Personal Stories of Moore's Law

The economics of Moore's Law first struck hit home for me in 1978. This was five years after leaving Massapequa to attend Rice. By this time, I was earning a Master's in Journalism at Northwestern. The school had paid for us to visit New York and be paraded before

---

42      CNBC covered the story of Intel's new fabrication plants https://www.cnbc.com/2021/03/23/intel-is-spending-20-billion-to-build-two-new-chip-plants-in-arizona.html

publishers like William Shawn of *The New Yorker*, before whose feet I sat, and *Newsweek*, which had a bar on top of its skyscraper called "Top of the Week."

I found some time and took a train back to Massapequa to see Tower TV. It had been replaced by a real estate office. (Last time I checked there was a Domino's Pizza there.)

Five years later, in 1983, I found myself climbing Peachtree Ridge in Atlanta toward a freelance assignment, carrying a 26-pound box that looked and felt just like the case of tubes I'd lugged on those service calls 15 years earlier.

This was my first computer, my Kaypro II. When the novelist Arthur C. Clarke died in 2008, his obituary pictured him behind the keyboard of his Kaypro II.[43] I bought mine at an Atlanta shop called "Hands-On Computers." I financed it. I had to. With its 300 baud Anchor Automation modem and dot-matrix C. Itoh printer, it cost almost $2,800. But it came with software.

The Kaypro would be my main machine for just two years.

The year before I bought the Kaypro, IBM had produced its own PC. The PC was incompatible with the Kaypro, it wouldn't run Kaypro programs, and it was only sold in large chain stores. It was more expensive and didn't include software.

There was another new machine coming into my life. Radio Shack had begun making the TRS-100, a four-pound machine with a tiny screen, measuring just 8 lines of 40 characters each, but a very sweet keyboard, perfect for taking notes and writing short stories. It even had a 300 baud modem for delivering them.

Over the decades I have had many computers, both laptops and desktops. I have never changed out machines because they stopped working, only because they became obsolete. The last picture tubes in

---

43      Here is a Clarke remembrance at Filmchat, showing him behind his Kaypro II. Mine looked just like it. https://www.patheos.com/blogs/filmchat/2008/03/arthur-c-clarke-1917-2008.html

my life disappeared around the time I wrote the first edition of this book, replaced by flat-screen monitors that are bigger. They were also much easier on the eyes.

In 2021 computers have been transformed by cloud computing into the equivalent of terminals, only with no moving parts. The final version of this book was edited on a Chromebook I bought at Costco for $149. The text lived in Google's cloud.

When it comes to the basic job of writing, the Kaypro II was perfectly adequate. The computer I use now hasn't made things that much easier. But there have been changes:

- I now look at black text on a white background instead of green text on a greener background.

- I can now store my entire life's work on a portable hard drive, a memory stick, or in the cloud.

- I now deliver my work via a broadband connection to the Internet in a few seconds, instead of printing it.

- The text of this book can download onto an Amazon Kindle in seconds.

But when it comes to putting words on "paper," I'm not much more productive than I was in the early 1980s.

I can now write on a beach instead of in my house. I prefer the house.

There are cloud-based services that will transcribe my interviews if I upload the digital sound files. How I wish I had them in 1979, when I went "clank clank" on an IBM Selectric at the Houston Business Journal, my phone headset on one shoulder, telling sources "I'm just taking a few notes" when I was transcribing their every word.

A lot more writing work is also consumed in the form of videos or podcasts rather than read. But videos must still be written, and podcasts at least need lists of questions.

It's amazing how similar my life in 2020 is to the life I led in 1983, when I first became a freelancer.

My kids have had to adapt to Moore's Law a lot more than I have.

## The Internet Generation

My daughter was born in 1988.

A few years later, when she was still in day care, I sat her down at my PC and set her to work "reviewing" pre-school software. Software in 1991 still came on floppy disks, loaded individually for set-up, then run from the PC's command line or c:/ prompt.

Her favorite was "*Fun with Letters and Words.*" She would press the "C" key, and the appropriate letter would appear on the screen. Press "C" twice and she would see a cat, and hear the word "cat," from the computer's speakers.

When my daughter was 6, I bought a Windows '95 machine that could run programs from a CD-ROM. One such program was "*Tuneland*," starring Howie Mandel, then an actor-comedian but now better known as a game show host. Now, when she clicked a mouse button, cartoon mice on the screen would dance and sing nursery rhymes. There was a game hidden on the disk, and as she clicked around characters would appear and then disappear.

My daughter was delighted. But sometimes she cried. Sometimes the computer would "crash," automatically rebooting itself but ending her game in the middle. At these times I would have to sit her down and tell her, "This is just late 20th century technology. In your time, things will be better."

I didn't know if she understood at the time. But she would.

In 2009 my daughter turned 21. By now she owned two very powerful PCs, one a laptop and the other a desktop. The flat screen monitor of her desktop PC doubled as a TV. The laptop had a wireless connection to the Internet which went through the wireless router next to my desk.

This meant my college-age daughter could sit on her bed, interacting with a Web site, while watching her favorite shows on the larger TV. She could connect or "sync" her personal files between the two machines. When she traveled to Italy for a summer semester, in 2008, she was able to find a wireless "hotspot" close to her room, in the medieval town of Montepulciano, and connect to the Internet at broadband speeds.

By 2019, computers were transparent to her. She is a child of the Internet era as I am a child of the TV era. She has grown up to see the Internet in the way I viewed television as a child. It's a natural part of her life. She doesn't phone home. She makes video calls using Skype, a Microsoft program linked to our email address.

Her life proves an important point. Our children are defining the Internet. My generation built it, hers masters it. Just as my father's generation didn't define TV, mine did. We understood TV's vocabulary and built our lives around that box. In the same way my daughter understands the Internet's vocabulary and builds her world around that.

What will my grandchildren build their worlds around?

## First PCs

Sometimes there are unexpected byproducts of Moore's Law. Sometimes it seems to make progress run backward.

I learned to type on a small Czech typewriter, which my father bought me for Christmas in 1963.

It came with a record called, I believe, *Learn to Type in an Hour*. Being 8 at the time, not knowing you can't learn how to type in an hour from a record, I did.

The whole set-up cost my dad $30. Sometimes I brought it to school with me. It's why and how I became a writer. From that day to this, I write every day. My dad bought it because my handwriting was atrocious. My teachers told him I wouldn't graduate elementary school with it. It still is terrible. The condition even has a name, dysgraphia.

My son was born in 1991. It was apparent early-on he was also dysgraphic, like his dad. Oh, good, I thought. Another writer in the family.

When he came to the same age I'd been with the Czech typewriter, however, portable manual typewriters no longer existed. He needed a $1,000 desktop PC. Fortunately, I had a program that could teach him to type just like that 1963 record, a program called *"Read, Write & Type."*

I thought this program would make my son a touch typist. Instead, he admitted later, he just played the game, without touch typing.

Worse, he couldn't bring his desktop computer to school, as I often did my typewriter. He got through with his lousy handwriting. He didn't begin writing in earnest until he went to graduate school and learned computer programming. His handwriting remains cramped, but he's a scientist, because writing is just one skill of a scientist.

Had he been born in 2001, I could have bought him a $400 "Netbook" for school, one with no moving parts, running the Linux operating system, and with free applications. Had he been born in 2011, I would be sending him to school with a $149 Chromebook, linked via WiFi to my own account in the cloud. He would not have to rely on his poor penmanship in class.

In the world of Moore's Law, where you stand depends on where you sit in time.

## LIFE LESSONS

My own life, and the lives of my children, hold important economic lessons, which have parallels in the stories of your life.

These lessons reflect the world as it has been redefined by Moore's Law.

Here are just a few:

- **Repair is a bad business**. As products get more complex, they become more reliable, not less reliable. It's much cheaper to replace a broken machine than to repair it.

- **Computers rot like fruit.** Had a school bought the computers my daughter first played with it would be unable to run the programs she had just two years later.

- **The cost of a new machine is not its retail price.** The cost of a new machine includes the money spent outfitting it, and the time spent learning to use it. In the age of iPhones and Androids, even this cost has been minimized.

- **Hardware is software.** Software defines what computers can do, and not all that software has to be on the machine in front of you.

- **The Network is the computer.** Clouds and networks now define computing. What you once called your computer is now just a user interface.

- **Not everything improves productivity.** Better isn't always easier.

- I'll bet you can think of a few more.

## ANALOG TO DIGITAL

The great revolutions in every industry happen as analog technology is replaced by digital computers or computer networks.

In the consumer electronics business, this happened in the 1960s. Even before integrated circuits came into vogue, when the equipment just consisted of transistors on circuit boards, reliability leapt ahead.

In office machines the big change came after the introduction of the

IBM PC in

1981 (although word processors and minicomputers had been around throughout the 1970s). Before that time computer terminals linked to large computers existed in many offices. But it was standard desktop PCs that made typewriters truly obsolete.

In time clouds would make even most offices obsolete.

# THE A-D CONVERSION

The process of full analog-to-digital conversion is often called "A-D Conversion." It took place in TV production in the early 1990s.

At that time digital editing suites that could produce broadcast-quality shows became available. Within two years this equipment was costing less than the analog equipment most TV producers had been using. Videotape and film are now doing a slow dissolve as digital video equipment follows the same path that editing took a decade ago.

The full "A-D Conversion" of TV broadcasting occurred in 2009, when digital TV channels completely replaced analog. Those with analog sets had to buy special "converter boxes" to see free over-the-air TV. In 2019 there are nearly 100 digital channels in Atlanta, although most are worthless. Most people didn't notice the A-D Conversion because they already had digital cable and cable set-ups. In 2019, everything is digital.

By 2010, anyone could create their own TV show, sometimes using a cell phone as a camera and edited on their home computer, then uploaded to a Web site like YouTube, to be seen by the world. YouTube videos and Internet databases helped elect President Barack Obama.

By 2016, the rise of social media technologies, Facebook, and Twitter, made these connections so cheap, and so ubiquitous, that America elected Donald Trump.

Technology does not deliver political utopia.

# The Cloud

Reading that last section from 2010, in 2019, startled me, because in less than a decade computing had become both invisible and ubiquitous, thanks to cloud computing.

Satellite and TV were just two of the casualties. So was video as it had previously existed. So were movies.

The technology that killed them was something that barely existed in 2010, streaming. By storing vast libraries of TV in cloud computers, delivering them individually to customers via fiber cables and wireless, clouds were able to replace broadcasting, even narrowcasting. Everyone gets to watch precisely what they want to watch, at any time.

The companies that built the biggest networks of cloud data networks were the most valuable in the world by 2019, worth nearly $1 trillion each. By 2021 Apple was worth $2 trillion, Microsoft $1.8 trillion. Amazon and Google, now called Alphabet, were worth $1.5 trillion each. Facebook, which didn't even exist in 2002, and China's Alibaba, founded in 1999 as a business-to-business marketplace, were both worth about $800 billion.

I call the five American companies the "Cloud Czars." They own today's Internet. Everyone else just rents.

Companies that rented cloud capacity dominated entertainment by 2019. Foremost among these, in the consumer space, was Netflix. What had begun as a business of mailing compact discs became, became a $200 billion streaming giant by the end of the decade, not just as big as a cable broadcasting company but as big as cable itself.

In 2010 the biggest sources of TV were Comcast, AT&T and Verizon. By 2021 they were Google's YouTube, Netflix, and Amazon. YouTube had an estimated audience of 1 billion, Netflix 200 million, Amazon 175 million. The cable and broadcast companies announced plans in late 2020 to try and catch up, Walt Disney launching Disney+, CBSViacom launching Paramount+, Comcast launching Peacock, and

AT&T launching HBO Max. Disney said in early 2021 it had 100 million subscribers. The rest were all below 40 million.[44]

Clouds also transformed software from a product bought in a store into a service you subscribed to from your desk. This made office supply stores like Staples and Office Depot practically disappear. The most complex applications are accessed from smartphones in 2019. Companies that didn't existed in the 20th century, with names like ServiceNOW and Workday, now have some of the world's most valuable database applications. A few older firms, like Adobe, were smart enough to jump on the cloud trend. Apple and Microsoft managed to become Cloud Czars by committing to the new model it in 2014 and 2016, respectively.

The number of casualties, however, was vast. IBM, which dominated computing for decades after it created the S/360 mainframe, was left behind. Oracle, whose databases were becoming a virtual monopoly in 2010, as it acquired the companies making its applications, was also left behind by mismanaging the cloud transition. So was AT&T, which instead chose to buy satellite and cable operations, and hand out dividends. All these companies are worth a small fraction of the larger cloud companies in 2021.

## TELEPHONY DISAPPEARS

Even in the mid-1990s it was believed that computers couldn't deliver the "five nines"

(99.99999) of reliability phone networks felt were needed to provide reliable service. Giant "Class V" switches from companies like Lucent and Nortel, larger than a refrigerator, were still the norm. These machines were based on computers, but they handled analog signals, and switched calls individually. Each line needed its own circuit board.

As I wrote the first edition of this book, in 2002, the "A-D Conversion" in this industry was well underway. Software based "soft"

44 I covered the streaming battle for Investorplace, an investment site, in March 2021. https://investorplace.com/2021/03/8-streaming-stocks-vying-to-be-king/

switches, some smaller than PCs, were replacing those older switches. Their capabilities could be changed simply by making changes in their software – no one need go near them. More important, the analog circuits on which the phone networks have been based for over 100 years were being replaced by digital networks, which handled voice calls as just one service among many.

By 2009 open source firms like Vyatta were offering free software that provided all the functions of Cisco routers, meaning a standard PC could replace the Internet switches that replaced those refrigerators of a decade earlier.

In 2021 voice is on its way out, a low bandwidth service. If you are doing an online meeting, it's usually video, a "Zoom" call. In 2019 over half of all phone calls consisted of automated, "spam" sales pitches. Communication has not only become fully digital, but largely asynchronous, performed at the convenience of each party rather than simultaneously, voice to voice or face to face.

The companies that provided those giant switches, Lucent, Nortel, and Alcatel, had all disappeared by 2019 inside Nokia, a rising cell phone giant in 2000 driven out of the business by the iPhone to become a wireless infrastructure company.

Meanwhile, the business that had been telephony was replaced by Internet systems from companies like Cisco Systems and Juniper Networks. The job of switching signals within cloud data centers was taken over by Mellanox, which was in turn acquired by Nvidia, a graphics computer chip company few people except video game enthusiasts had heard of 10 years before.

Moore's Law hastens corporate evolution, too.

## SIDE-EFFECTS OF THE A-D CONVERSION

The early 20th century economist Joseph Schumpeter coined a term for this process, "creative destruction,"[45] In the world of Moore's Law it

---

45      Here is Wikipedia's article on Schumputer https://en.wikipedia.org/wiki/

is accelerating like a rocket lifting-off from a launchpad.

Joseph Heller, in his 1961 novel Catch-22[46], offered a memorable description and put it in the hands of Milo Minderbinder, an avaricious war profiteer. When something was wrecked, he would simply say "Think of it as evolution in action."

The simplest implication of creative destruction is obvious. What happens to the people and businesses supporting the old systems? The same thing that happened to Tower TV -- they go away. Trying to save them is a waste of time. My dad became a locksmith and maintained his skills as a small businessman almost to the day he died, in 1999. You adapt.

It's not always enough to replace one kind of store with another, selling a different product. Economic models must also adapt constantly. Moore's Law means that, once the "A-D Conversion" is finished within an industry, its evolution has just begun. After the conversion equipment will get cheap fast, it will get better fast, and it will also become more reliable fast. The pace of change accelerates, and even those who anticipate its beginning are not safe from the implications.

Computer retailing has undergone a half-dozen transformations over the course of my working life, eventually becoming transpoarent.

The stores that replaced "Hands-On Computers" in the mid-1980s, like ComputerLand, were replaced within a few years by "computer superstores" such as CompUSA.

But those stores, too, were soon having to compete head-to-head with consumer electronics stores and giant retailers such as Wal-Mart, which drove many out of business

Even these stores had a hard time competing in the 1990s against Dell Computer, which sold PCs directly and didn't buy the parts needed to build one until it had an order to sell one.

By 2009 even the most efficient computer retailers were finding it

Joseph_Schumpeter

46      Catch-22 came out the same year as M*A*S*H and has been overshadowed by it. https://en.wikipedia.org/wiki/Catch-22

hard to profitably stock $400 Netbooks.

The entire distribution channel was now online, as was the media covering it.

By 2019 it's all changed again.

If you want a PC, you just use your smartphone to order it from Amazon. It will be at your desk in a day. Or you can go to a warehouse store like Costco and pick a "Chromebook," built for the cloud and running a Google-made operating system based on its browser, for $150. The PC has become what Gordon Moore envisioned in his original article, a black box bought by the notions.

At each stage of this one industry's evolution, there has been tremendous dislocation. Businesses built around one business model went under, and their replacements didn't last much longer. People who worked in the old computer stores had to find new work, in education, writing software, or working within corporations that had lots of computers. Many left the PC industry entirely.

There is no way to stop any of this, any more than the Luddites[47] could stop the automation of textiles in the first decades of the 19th century.

## WHAT COMES NEXT?

Moore's Law turns the economy over repeatedly. Intelligence now lives in your doorbell, in the office lights, in most factory machines, in all sorts of things we never thought needed intelligence. There's now an even bigger shift taking place, as these intelligent machines are connected in new ways and start communicating with one another. The trend can be summed up in this way:

1. The Steam Engine of the 18th Century automated production.

2. The Railroad of the 19th Century automated transport

---

47      I talk about Luddites a lot. Here is Wikipedia's description of them. https://en.wikipedia.org/wiki/Luddite

3. The Computer of the 20th Century automated intelligence.

4. The Networks of the 21st Century automate living.

What computer networks did for stocks and bonds in the 1990s is now happening everywhere. That's how the Internet will really change the future. When every machine around us has gained intelligence, and everyone is connected, then the costs of buying and selling drift toward zero, thanks to Moore's Law.

I wrote 20 years ago that there was "a lot Moore" to come.

I was righter than I realized.

# Chapter 4

# Moore and Hardware

Gordon Moore didn't set out to change the world. He only set out to describe one part of it, the part he was working on, the integrated circuit.

That idea, that circuit lines could grow closer indefinitely, has obvious limits. We were approaching them even as I wrote the first version of this book. As the distance between circuit lines narrowed, the process of narrowing them further grew more complex.

Moore himself is a precision-based scientist-engineer. He saw all this coming and sought to amend his law while accepting the Presidential Medal of Freedom in 2002. "Hooking up billions of transistors on a chip is something that could space out the performance doubling eventually to every four or five years. We're starting to shrink [chips] less rapidly than in the past," he said.[48]

I'm a huge fan of Gordon Moore but focusing solely on changes in chip density underestimates the impact of his revolution. Focusing only on silicon chips, and not on related technologies whose improvements are enabled by chips, also underestimates his revolution.

## Moore was a Pessimist

With all due respect, I believe Gordon Moore was a pessimist. But there is good reason for his pessimism.

For Intel, the Pentium IV chip was a turning point in the history of Moore's Law.

Pentium IV chips were physically larger than the 80386 chips made in the mid-1980s, and their "sockets," through which they connected to circuit boards, were bigger, too. More important, as electricity ran

48      What Mr. Moore said is true, but the progress of Moore's Law goes in many different directions. https://www.eetimes.com/document.asp?doc_id=1133402#

through these chips, heat built up. This made the chips less reliable.

Intel, which Gordon Moore helped found and which he led, made two important decisions in 2006:

1. Intel decided to switch exclusively to "low power" chip designs[49], abandoning designs used for desktops for those used in notebooks and smaller devices.

2. Intel began producing "dual core" chips, putting 2, then 4, and finally more computers on each chip, complete with their own memory and processing.[50]

These two innovations allowed Intel, and rivals, to keep improvements coming. By 2008 Intel had chips with circuit lines 35 nanometers apart. By 2018 it was producing circuits 14 nanometers apart, and rival Taiwan Semiconductor was preparing to deliver 7 nanometer designs.

The slowing pace of circuit lines approaching one another had some writing "Moore's Law is dead." Yet chips keep getting better and better, faster, and faster.

For me, microprocessors are just one small piece of the Moore's Law story. There are always knock-on effects that drive change ever faster. Here are some in computer hardware:

- **Memory chips** are becoming faster, with more memory, for less money, using less power. In 2001 I wrote about memory chips measured in kilobytes. In 2010 I talked megabytes. In 2020 standard smartphones contain 64 Gigabytes of storage.

- **New designs** let chips get faster without putting more circuits

---

49      I was sad to see this story at C|Net https://www.cnet.com/news/intel-powers-up-plans-for-low-power-chips-1/
50      Here is how C|Net covered the dual core story https://www.cnet.com/news/new-intel-quad-core-chips-are-really-double-duo-cores/

on each one. Multi-core designs are just one example of this trend. Optimizing the design for a specific purpose, like Nvidia graphics, can create entirely new industries like artificial intelligence.

- **Circuit boards** keep getting better. Speed an electron's path around a board and you've got a faster computer even if the microprocessor itself doesn't change.

- **Combining components** can add up to a huge improvement in the speed and reliability of a product and lower its cost. Your phone contains dozens of products that were once sold separately, from cameras and flashlights to radios, TVs and recording devices. With each generation of equipment more functions are combined onto fewer chips.

- **Clients and Clouds.** The rise of clouds means client devices need less memory. Today almost all the memory on desktops and in phones is done in memory chips rather than spinning hard drives.

In 2020 it's clearer than ever that Gordon Moore was a pessimist. Following is a brief history of how we got here.

## New Types of Chips

With each generation of microprocessors chips, there are new opportunities to improve other types of chips as well, making them faster, less expensive, and more reliable than the chips which came before. This acts as a multiplier effect on Moore's Law.

But there are other types of innovations in integrated circuits beyond just bringing circuit lines together.

# RISC Chips

The Reduced Instruction Set Computer (RISC) chip was one of the first such advances I covered, way back in the 1980s.

The "father" of the RISC design, an IBM engineer named John Cocke, [51] found that he could speed up chips by simply reducing the number of different arithmetic functions each chip had to support. Cocke broke down complex instructions into sets of simpler ones and delivered a huge increase in processing speed.

Within a very few years so-called Complex Instruction Set Computers (CISC) were on their way out, although the debate of RISC vs. CISC continues.[52]

## Asynchronous Computing

Another innovation was to eliminate the clock on a chip. On early chips instructions were performed in sequence, usually 8 bits at a time. A 16-bit chip could handle twice as wide a track of data, 32-bit chips twice as much as that.

But what about just eliminating the clock and letting processors work how they wished?

Ivan Sutherland, a researcher at Sun Microsystems (acquired by Oracle Corp. in 2010), said in 2002 that chip speeds could be drastically increased by letting each part of the chip work at its own pace. He called this "asynchronous computing,"[53] distinguishing it from designs where all the chip's functions are synchronized through the on-board clock.

51    The New York Times eulogized Mr. Cocke in 2002 https://www.nytimes. com/2002/07/19/business/john-cocke-a-chip-wizard-from-ibm-is-dead-at-77.html
52    Here is a brief description of the differences between CISC and RISC. https://medium.com/@csoham358/a-beginners-guide-to-risc-and-cisc-architectures-fc9af424db3b

53    Asynchronous computing does not depend on a chip's clock. Things run when they run, as this article in *Scientific American* shows. https://www. scientificamerican.com/article/computers-without-clocks-2002-07-15

Researchers in Japan, England and the U.S. quickly designed chips using this idea, and Sun's UltraSparc III chip, used some asynchronous circuits.

## PROBABILISTIC COMPUTING

Another route to speed is "probabilistic" computing, first developed at IBM in software during the 1980s. While math problems demand absolute accuracy, people don't think that way. In 2002 Krishna Palem at Rice University suggested that getting part of an answer right, calculating Pi as 3.14 rather than 3.14016, for instance, could speed a chip's decision-making, and by 2008 this idea came to be taken seriously.[54] He called such chips "probabilistic complementary metal oxide semiconductor technology" (PC-MOS).

By using such human-like concepts as estimating and "good enough" imaging, probabilistic chips can reach conclusions faster, using less power than other chips.[55] Such chips can also be made with a higher yield, because those with minor defects don't have to be tossed aside.

Probabilistic computing, whether described in hardware or software, may be the next step in artificial intelligence, allowing machines to "estimate" answers from limited evidence just like we do.[56]

## QUANTUM COMPUTING

Moore's Law, as originally written, does have physical limits. Atoms can only come so close to one another. But what if you could store and manipulate data within the structure of an atom?

Perhaps the best proof that Moore was a pessimist is quantum

---

54 *Technology Review* had a good article on probabilistic computing. http://www2.technologyreview.com/news/409597/tr10-probabilistic-chips/
55 *Extreme Tech* described how probabilistic computing can improve performance https://www.extremetech.com/computing/168348-probabilistic-computing-imprecise-chips-save-power-improve-performance
56 *Phys.Org* described the use of estimating in artificial intelligence applications. https://phys.org/news/2018-05-probabilistic-artificial-intelligence.html

computing. [57] First proposed by theoretical physicist Richard Feynman and Russian mathematician Yuri Manin in the 1980s, the idea is that the quantum state of an atom can be measured, its electromagnetic field defined as a 1 or 0, and then, just like a light bulb, used to make computations. This quantum state is called a qubit, short for quantum bit.

The first two-qubit quantum device was developed at the University of Bristol, in England, in 2018[58], and Intel has put such a device onto a silicon chip.[59] While Intel also claimed to have a 49-qubit device by 2019 [60], measuring qubits on silicon brings them much closer to market.

Hartmut Neven, director of Google's Quantum Computing Lab, has created a new rule to describe what is happening. Sometimes it's called "Neven's Law." [61]

Neven's Law is that a quantum computer can deliver double exponential growth, not just the exponential growth found in Moore's Law. What could this mean in practice? In December 2018 Google scientists were able to model a calculation running on their latest quantum chip using a laptop. A month later the same simulation took a more powerful desktop computer. By February, the researchers required time on Google's own cloud to run their simulation. By the end of that month, the simulations were requiring a million processors.

---

57 Here is a Wikipedia piece on quantum computing. https://en.wikipedia.org/wiki/Quantum_computing
58 *Cosmos Magazine* described the Bristol quantum computer. https://cosmosmagazine.com/technology/two-qubit-chip-draws-quantum-computing-closer
59 *The Next Web* covered Intel's discovery at https://thenextweb.com/science/2018/02/16/intel-just-put-a-quantum-computer-on-a-silicon-chip/
60 *Extreme Tech* covered this Intel breakthrough. https://www.extremetech.com/computing/261734-intel-unveils-new-quantum-computer-declares-quantum-breakthrough
61 Neven's Law puts Moore's Law into the equivalent of Tesla's "ludicrous speed." https://www.quantamagazine.org/does-nevens-law-describe-quantum-computings-rise-20190618

This is important because the problems scientists are considering are also growing more complex, and at a quantum rate.[62] Researchers at CalTech and MIT recently said the number of hard-to-solve but easy-to-verify problems in science is also growing exponentially.[63] Quantum computers are required to find these answers.

## PROGRAMMABLE LOGIC DEVICES

Another way to increase the speed with which things happen inside a computer (and to make all sorts of new computerized devices possible) is to combine software and processing on a single chip.

Such chips are called Programmable Logic Devices. [64]They are loaded with software during the manufacturing process. They may have a single function, and be able to run just a single program, but they allow any product to become miniaturized, and let designers add intelligence to them.

There are many kinds of PLDs, and electrical engineers are always tweaking the state-of-the-art. They make computing invisible to the user. The operating system and applications are all hard-wired.

One of my favorite types of PLD in 2002 was the Field Programmable Gate Array (FPGA), [65] which can not only hold programs in memory, but the logic gates needed to run the program. These dramatically reduce the amount of time it took to bring a product to market, while reducing a product's size and power consumption

Other types of PLDs include Programmable Array Logic (PAL) chips, whose fuses are "blown apart" to define their function, Application

62 There is no limit to the need for computing power, as Quanta Magazine wrote in 2019 https://www.quantamagazine.org/computer-scientists-expand-the-frontier-of-verifiable-knowledge-20190523/

63 More on the need for quantum computers. https://www.quantamagazine.org/computer-scientists-expand-the-frontier-of-verifiable-knowledge-20190523/

64     Here is Wikipedia's article on Programmable Logic Devices https://en.wikipedia.org/wiki/Programmable_logic_device

65     FGPAs have now been around for almost 20 years, as Wikipedia notes https://en.wikipedia.org/wiki/Field-programmable_gate_array

Specific Integrated Circuits (ASICs),[66] which have software "burned-in" to them at the fab, and Complex PLDs (CPLDs),[67] which have elements common to both PALs and FGPAs.

## MOLECULAR MEMORY

Silicon oxide isn't the only molecule that can be used to store information. As circuit lines on microprocessors grew closer together, memory was becoming the "weakest link" in the race to provide processing speed. If data can't be fed in-and-out of the chip as fast as the chip can process it, then it doesn't matter how fast the chip gets – the work gets done only as fast as the slowest chip in the stack. Faster memory lets you use the speed of faster microprocessors.

Multi-core designs help with this, by having memory on-the-chip, close to where it's being processed. But these chips must still have their memory refreshed often, and this can slow down an entire system. By the time I began my first re-write of this book, in 2010, this was becoming a big problem.

Ferroelectric Random-Access Memory (FerroRAM), as a concept, was first proposed in 1952. By 2009 Toshiba delivered a FerroRAM chip capable of transferring data at a rate of 1.6 GBytes per second. [68]

NASA scientists were still studying the concept of molecular memory in 2018, focusing on long-term storage needed for interplanetary flight, and organic compounds for storing data. [69] There has also been research into using graphene, a form of pure carbon, for storing data.[70]

---

66      Wikipedia describes ASICs here. https://en.wikipedia.org/wiki/Application-specific_integrated_circuit
67      Yes, another Wikipedia article. But the addresses of such articles don't move https://en.wikipedia.org/wiki/Complex_programmable_logic_device
68      Phys.Org described this chip in 2009. https://phys.org/news/2009-02-toshiba-world-highest-bandwidth-highest-density.html
69      Here is the NASA article. https://www.nasa.gov/centers/ames/research/technology-onepagers/nonvolatile_memory.html
70      Humblebrag. Much of the theoretical work on graphene was done at my alma mater, Rice University. https://www.nanowerk.com/spotlight/spotid=22630.php

# New Circuit Boards

In addition to building new chips, Moore's Law can be extended with new ways to assemble chips into products.

When I was helping to fix TVs, back in the 1960s, we always kept a soldering iron and some solder in the bottom of the tube case, a cardboard box with two side panels that opened from the top, revealing a collection of tools below. Ironically, it was about the same size and weight of the Kaypro II computer I would buy in the early 1980s.

Solder is a metal alloy used to join other metals. The word comes from medieval English, and originally referred to the material used between the glass in stained glass windows.

The most popular form of solder used at Tower TV in the 1960s was a mixture with lead. Lead melted at low temperatures. The soldering iron melted the solder, which flowed until it hardened in the air, away from the source of heat. When I close my eyes, I can still smell the lead melting and see it bubble around its central tube of resin.

Back then we applied solder in one of two ways. If we thought the problem was a break in the circuit on the bottom of the board, where the "wires" were metal and the spaces between plastic, we'd flow solder along the path of the circuit to repair the break. If a part on top of the board was being replaced, we'd either snip the ends of the part and connect the new one to the wires or (more often) simply solder the new part directly on the old leads. Most of these circuits were made of a plastic called mylar, with copper underneath, laid on top of a stiff plastic (sometimes even cardboard) board.

But lead is poisonous and it's not a great conductor. Other solder materials were already being developed in the 1960s. If you look inside an inkjet printer, for instance, you'll see a little circuit made of copper and polyester. This circuit board was made through a process called electroplating, allowing it to be more flexible.

Various combinations of metal-on-plastic were still being used to create PCs in the 1980s. To make repair easier, chips were made with metal pins that plugged into plastic connectors. Each receptacle had metal in it and the whole socket, in turn, was soldered to the bottom of the circuit board. Back when expensive, 8 Kbit memory chips were the norm, boards were often shipped with some empty connectors. Users like me would buy chips when we could afford them, plugging them into the sockets through the connectors. (Be careful not to bend the pins!)

By changing the ways in which circuit boards were made – using better conductors (such as gold) and simpler manufacturing techniques (like plastic laminates), computer makers could boost the machine's performance, even reduce costs, and lower power requirements.

The biggest bottleneck in computers is always when data moves between chips. After all, even if your neighbor's bathroom is on the other side of the wall behind your head, you'll still get to your TV across the room faster than to the toilet behind it.

## COLLABORATION

Every advance anywhere in the process of making chips or putting them together into products can speed things up, improve reliability, and make it easier to turn fast chips into neat products. Little steps add up to huge leaps.

I call this the "YMCA effect," because the trainers at my local "Y" are always harping on it.

You make little improvements, day after day, and they add up.

When I started an exercise program in my 40s, I was barely able to stay on a treadmill for 30 minutes at a speed of 4.2 miles per hour. But I went to that treadmill every day. Six months later I was shocked when the treadmill slowed down by itself as I was going 6 miles per hour. It turned out I'd reached the program's suggested limit of 400 calories per workout. (I wish I could still do that in my 60s, but human bodies aren't subject to Moore's Law.)

There are a lot of disciplines associated with the design of microprocessors and computer equipment. They were explained to me in 2007 by an executive with Applied Materials, a leading maker of chip-making equipment.

He pointed out to me how many different disciplines go into making faster chips:

- Chemistry to come up with new chip materials.
- Molecular science to find new ways to use these materials.
- Software engineering to come up with new ways to design microprocessors, and
- Electrical engineering to pull chips together into products.

Since we spoke it's the third discipline, software engineering, that has become the key to faster chip designs. Hardware has become software.

There's yet another additive effect to Moore's Law, produced by the market.

## COMPETITION

Competition exists in every single niche within the semiconductor industry. And competition isn't limited to industry. Colleges and universities compete fiercely for research grants and other aid, often by raiding one another's faculty for new stars. Major research centers in Europe, Asia and North America compete with one another for breakthroughs. Science and engineering are very competitive businesses.

What this adds up to is progress. We test ourselves and we test each other. Someone gets there first, but in the process, everyone wins.

# THE NETWORK EFFECT

The rise of the Internet has created yet-another way to increase the speed of technology's advance.

By publishing new findings first on their Web sites, publications like the *Journal of the American Medical Association* have not only transformed themselves, but science itself. Science can no longer wait the three months needed to publish and distribute new findings. Now findings are "published" as soon as the editors review them.

Sometimes they are published before. Since 2001, almost 14,000 "open access" academic journals have been created, some using techniques of "crowd-sourcing" to test articles. These journals are listed as Directory of Open Access Journals.[71]

The idea of a monthly publication schedule became a thing of the past thanks to the Internet. I had a tiny hand in this, launching the *Interactive Age Daily* in late 1994, at CMP Media. The Daily was the first daily coverage of the Internet, on the Internet, and debuted along with the print magazine on October 26, 1994. Its wide popularity spurred the creation of "Web-only" media sites like News.com, which dominated coverage of the computer industry for a decade, and Slashdot, a news-discussion site specializing in open source.

By 2018, the technology news industry had transformed again, with new leaders that emerged from the blog metaphor I'd worked on at *ZDNet* from 2005-2010. Sites like *Mashable*, *The Verge*, and *Recode* were able to quickly establish themselves, because the Web is open to innovation.

Yet the Web, too, is the tip of a larger iceberg. I first got involved with the online world in 1986, when I went to an early meeting of the Electronic Networking Association. This was an international group built around computer conferencing technology. In 1989 I even traveled to the Japanese city of Sendai for an ENA conference.

The network effect, applied to science, technology, and the

---

71      You can find the DOAJ here https://doaj.org/

development of the microprocessor, has been in constant acceleration since the Internet itself was launched. That came with a data call between UCLA and Stanford Research Institute,[72] in 1969, a year before the Intel 4004 chip went on the market.

Since then, the growth of the Internet has been a multiplier in the history of Moore's Law. More like Neven's Law. (That's called a callback.)

## What's a Cloud?

When I wrote my first edition of this book, in 2002, Google was a start-up. By the time I revised it, in 2010, Google was a public company. Today it is one of the five most valuable companies in the world, a "Cloud Czar." Each Czar is built with a computer technology that didn't exist in 2001, the cloud.

Clouds are based on four concepts:

» Distributed computing

» Virtual operating systems

» Open source software

» Low-cost commodity hardware

## Distributed Computing

The idea behind distributed computing is simple, and dates from the 1960s.[73] It became its own branch of computer science in the 1980s.

72      The UCLA-Stanford event was described here https://en.wikipedia.org/wiki/History_of_the_Internet.

73      This is according to Wikipedia https://en.wikipedia.org/wiki/Distributed_computing#History.

The idea is simple. Take a huge computing task, one that no single computer can possibly handle on its own and divide it up into smaller chunks. Distribute these chunks of data, along with a processing program, to thousands of other computers. When a computer is done with its chunk, it sends the results back, and gets another chunk. Even with the time taken dividing the task, passing it around, and collecting the results, the answer still comes back faster.

Some of the first systems I saw were just stacks of Macintosh computers with wires coming out of the back, the distribution and collection of data done by software.

The first large-scale distributed computing project I participated in was SETI@Home,[74] launched in 1998 at the University of California in Berkeley. The idea was to analyze the huge amount of random data being received by the Arecibo antenna in Puerto Rico [75], which was trying to find if there might be intelligent life on other planets. Over 3.8 million people participated in the project, which involved downloading and running a "screensaver" program while their own PCs were not in active use, using over 1 million years of computer time.

In 2005, Intel decided to start using this concept in the design of its own chips. Since the first "dual-core" chip was released, the concept has gone mainstream and is used in chips other than microprocessors.[76]

## VIRTUALIZATION

Virtualization has been around, as a concept, since the 1960s, but it didn't explode onto the market until after VMware launched its patented VMware virtual platform for Intel-based computers in 2001. [77]

---

74      You can date your own age by whether you used SETI@Home when you were a kid. https://setiathome.berkeley.edu/
75      Aricibo collapsed in late 2020. The film is very sad to see but was covered by *Nature Magazine.* https://www.nature.com/articles/d41586-020-03421-y
76      Here is Wikipedia's article on multi-core processors. https://en.wikipedia.org/wiki/Multi-core_processor
77      Wikipedia now offers a timeline on the development of virtualization. https://en.wikipedia.org/wiki/Timeline_of_virtualization_development

Here too, the concept it simple. A virtual operating system sits on top of a program's own operating system, so that program can share space on a larger collection of hardware.

Virtualization isn't just used to combine computers, but to let general purpose computers perform more-specialized tasks. Virtual memory systems, virtual filing, and virtual networking systems have taken market share from specialized devices in recent years, transforming entire sectors of the computer business.

Virtual machines have been followed, in the last decade, with "containerization." A program, its data, and all the other resources needed for it to run are loaded as a virtual "container" within a larger system, the way containers are stacked along a train or in a ship. The first such system, named "Hadoop"[78] after the plush elephant toy of programmer Doug Cutting's child.[79] It was originally used to support MapReduce, a Google algorithm for speeding search. Sadly, while Hadoop was a great technology it was not a huge commercial success. [80]

## OPEN SOURCE

Open source, described by Eric Raymond in his collection of essays, *The Cathedral and the Bazaar*, [81] holds that getting more eyes on software is more productive than holding development within a single company. It was derived from an earlier concept. Free and Open Source Software (FOSS), created by the Free Software Foundation (FSF) under its founder, Richard Stallman.

The most popular open source license is the General Public License

---

78    Here is Apache's page on Hadoop https://hadoop.apache.org/
79    I was fortunate enough to interview Doug Cutting at an open source conference. This article isn't from that. http://www.balasubramanyamlanka.com/history-of-hadoop/
80    Teradata blogged about Hadoop's failure as I was updating this book. https://www.teradata.com/Blogs/Why-Hadoop-Failed-and-Where-We-Go-from-Here
81    The Cathedral and the Bazaar is one of the classic books in computing. https://en.wikipedia.org/wiki/The_Cathedral_and_the_Bazaar

(GPL) 2.0 [82], created by the FSF. But there are other GPLs meant to cover different market conditions. There are also many so-called Berkeley Software Distribution (BSD) Licenses,[83] which are said to be more market oriented.

When I began work at *ZDNet* in 2005 the concept of open source was very controversial. Today Microsoft, one of those early critics, is an open source advocate and owns the largest open source repository, GitHub.

Stallman, known by his initials, RMS, was always controversial. A scandal involving his comments on a sex scandal involving Jeffrey Epstein forced him off the FSF board in 2019.[84] When he was returned to the board in 2021, the move was so controversial it seemed the FSF itself might collapse. My friend Steven J. Vaughan-Nichols covered the story. [85]

The key to open source is that its benefits flow mainly to users, not developers. This is a feature, not a bug, and has long caused consternation in the development community, leading to business models like open-core,[86] in which only limited versions of the program are open source.

It also led to an all-out revolt against open source by Oracle.

After buying Sun Microsystems in 2010, Oracle chose to copyright the Application Program Interfaces describing how it was made and, when Google used them anyway, it sued. The case bounced around the court for a decade until early 2021, when the Supreme Court ruled 6-2 in

---

82      GPL 2.0 remains the most popular open source license. https://www.gnu.org/licenses/old-licenses/gpl-2.0.en.html
83      Here is Wikipedia's article on BSD licenses. https://en.wikipedia.org/wiki/BSD_licenses
84      Wikipedia has a long article on Stallman. https://en.wikipedia.org/wiki/Richard_Stallman
85      It's sad when the people associated with a work are personally discredited. I don't think it should discredit the work, but in this case it might. https://www.zdnet.com/article/return-of-stallman-to-fsf-sparks-outrage-among-open-source-and-free-software-leaders/
86      The idea of open core has proven to be almost as controversial as Stallman. Here is Wikipedia's article on it. https://en.wikipedia.org/wiki/Open-core_model

favor of Google. [87] Unfortunately, the result doesn't settle the question of whether APIs can turn open source closed. The court decided to address it, basing its decision on the idea that Google had made "fair use" of the API.

The biggest users of open source software today are cloud companies. In addition to the Linux operating system, companies like Amazon. Com, Microsoft, Google, Facebook, and Apple support many other open source projects through foundations like the Linux Foundation [88] serving the Linux operating system and Apache, [89] originally created to support a web server.

## COMMODITY HARDWARE

The fourth key to cloud costs is low-cost commodity hardware. Don't use the fastest cheap. Use the cheapest one, and use a lot of them.

Back in the $20^{th}$ century, the way to get a faster computer was to use a faster microprocessor, or other fast parts.

Distributed computing and virtualization changed the equation.

Instead of buying a faster computer, cloud companies built super-fast systems with cheap hardware. This was combined with open source, as in Facebook's Open Compute Project[90] and Netflix' Open Connect,[91] aimed at sharing other cost-cutting ideas.

Cloud computing systems today consist of racks-and-racks of commodity servers, often connected via fiber cables, located in huge warehouses far from any city. Where there are enough of these centers, as in northern Virginia, new cloud factory towns have developed.

There is also a big industry in connecting these clouds with each

---

87      Here is the 2021 Supreme Court decision. https://www.supremecourt.gov/opinions/20pdf/18-956_d18f.pdf
88      The Linux Foundation is at http://www.linux.org
89      The Apache Foundation is at https://www.apache.org/
90      The Open Compute Foundation is at https://www.opencompute.org/
91      The Open Connect Foundation is at https://openconnect.netflix.com/en/

other, and with the smaller systems operated by private companies, called "private clouds." Companies are rebuilding their internal systems on cloud standards and connecting them, via these centers, to the largest public clouds, creating what are called "hybrid clouds."

All this has helped make cloud, which was still developing in 2010, the dominant computing paradigm of 2020. As cloud companies develop artificial intelligence applications and voice interfaces like Amazon's Alexa, which require faster processing speed than even commodity clouds provide, they are beginning to upgrade their clouds with specialized graphics hardware.

Change, even in the cloud, is constant.

The "network effect" of Moore's Law, then, involves connecting people, connecting machines, and having machines work together. It's accelerating the pace of scientific change in every direction.

## The Impact on Productivity

In 2002, with stock markets tanking, war drums beating, and economic growth slowing to a crawl, it may have been hard to recognize just how powerful the revolution of Moore's Law had become, and to see its forward momentum.

In the manufacturing era economists measured this through productivity. Productivity is the amount of work the average worker can do in an hour, using the average amount of automation supplied them. The more productive you are, the more work you can do in a day, and the more you can earn from your work.

Productivity growth often lags automation. It takes time to learn how to use a new machine, and it takes time for managers to apply innovation into their business process. In the first few years or months after a new system comes in, productivity may go down as people go up the learning curve.

For many years this frustrated economists. In 1987 economist

Robert Solow of MIT [92], who turned 95 in 2019, commented, "We see the computer age everywhere but in the productivity statistics."

This has since changed.

During the last quarter of 2001, at the bottom of the "dot-bomb" recession, productivity rose at an annual rate of 5.5%, according to the Labor Department. Even while U.S. businesses were laying-off hundreds of thousands of people, they were able to produce more goods and services.

This has continued, and in fact has accelerated. This is not always reflected in productivity statistics because computers can become so productive that human beings are no longer necessary. In the years after the dot-bomb thousands of middle management jobs, people who moved information within organizations, disappeared, replaced by database software applications. In the years after the 2008-2009 "Great Recession" many sales jobs disappeared, replaced by Web sites.

Moore's Law has allowed productivity to increase even while energy use has been held steady. [93] The link between energy use and production has been broken.[94]

The bottom line is this. The gating factor to global growth today is human capital, talented, trained, motivated human minds.

It's not a miracle. It's Moore's Law in action.

It will keep working as far ahead as we can see.

---

92      Wikipedia has an article about Solow at https://en.wikipedia.org/wiki/Robert_Solow
93      The relative efficiency of computing has caused utilities to embrace electric cars https://www.eia.gov/todayinenergy/detail.php?id=33812
94      The McKinsey report on energy and productivity is an important document, at https://www.mckinsey.com/industries/electric-power-and-natural-gas/our-insights/the-decoupling-of-gdp-and-energy-growth-a-ceo-guide

# Chapter 5

# Moore and the Internet

The first Intel microprocessor and the Internet came along at about the same time.

But they didn't grow up in lockstep.

Partly this was a deliberate government policy. Commercial use of the Internet was prohibited until the mid-1990s.

Partly this was due to how computing developed. During the 1970s and 1980s, the edge of what would become the Internet developed faster than the core. Local networking developed under the Ethernet standard, created during the early 1970s by Robert Metcalfe[95] at Xerox PARC, a California think tank that also came up with the graphical user interface and computer mouse.

Local networks connected desktop PCs to servers located within the same buildings. The primary program used for this was NetWare, from Novell, first released in 1983.[96] In the 1980s, networking within buildings had what seemed like broad highways running between computers, while outside there were the equivalent of dirt tracks.

While NetWare worked, however, it was built for IBM-compatible PCs, and thus lacked a graphical user interface, or GUI, often pronounced "gooey." Most PC technical development during the 1980s focused on finding a GUI that would work on the PC.

## Interfaces

The user interface defines your productivity.

---

95      When I first began reporting online in 1985, Robert Metcalfe was a very big name. https://www.thoughtco.com/history-of-ethernet-robert-metcalfe-4079022

96      Netware is now little more than a Wikipedia article. In the 1980s, it was hugely important. https://en.wikipedia.org/wiki/NetWare

The first computer I used had punch cards. It was a DEC PDP-8, and it sat in the basement of a Rice University academic building called Herman Brown Hall in the mid-1970s. To use it a program would be typed, line-by-line, onto the cards, which were filled with holes that were emptied out or "punched" on this command. I would tie them together with a rubber band and offer them through a window to an operator. The operator would read the "deck" of cards through a punch card "reader" into the machine, which would respond, after a while, with a print-out. In my case, this print-out was usually a very short one, indicating I had made a mistake in Line 3 of my program.

Punch cards pre-dated the computer, having been developed in the 1880s, and used first in the 1890 census. For 50 years, computing consisted of entering data onto cards and sorting them into stacks. [97]

The idea of speeding up this process with a screen was already 20 years old by the time I got to Rice. A version was shown in the 1957 film "Desk Set,"[98] starring Spencer Tracy and Katherine Hepburn. Workers typed questions at a typewriter, in front of TV screen, and received answers through a print-out.

The late Douglas Engelbart added the mouse in the mid-1960s.[99] His team at the Stanford Research Institute did more than that. To make the mouse accurate they created a "bit map" of the screen, His team's oNLine System (NLS) featured all the hallmarks of later operating systems. The mouse itself was patented in 1967.[100]

The first Graphical User Interface[101] was perfected in the 1970s, through a team at Xerox' Palo Alto Research Center headed by Alan Kay. The GUI let the mouse act on any point in the bitmap. The GUI

97 Wikipedia has a page on the Hollerith machine, including a photo of a tabulator and sorting box, at https://en.wikipedia.org/wiki/Tabulating_machine
98 The user interface in Desk Set, the computer speaking while emitting printouts and users typing questions, was fictional. https://en.wikipedia.org/wiki/Desk_Set
99 Douglas Engelbart's Wikipedia page. https://en.wikipedia.org/wiki/Douglas_Engelbart
100 Engelbart's demonstration of a mouse combined with a graphical user interface in 1968 is now referred to as the "Mother of all Demos." https://en.wikipedia.org/wiki/The_Mother_of_All_Demos
101 Early GUIs are described by Wikipedia at https://en.wikipedia.org/wiki/Graphical_user_interface#Early_efforts

was made the user interface for a computer language called Smalltalk. The result was a 1973 computer called the Xerox Alto [102], which never reached production.

To become a mass market product, the GUI needed Moore's Law to develop enough computer power, in a small enough form factor, at a low enough price, to create a mass market for its software and applications. This was what Apple did, first with the Lisa in 1983, then with a less-expensive computer called the Macintosh. The Mac was introduced in 1984 with a brilliant commercial that was shown only once, during that year's Super Bowl telecast.[103] In the process Apple abandoned their old interface, Apple DOS. Users had to abandon their old Apple II hardware to use the Apple Macintosh.

Apple's Macintosh had the graphical computer market to itself for the rest of the decade. It bifurcated the tech world, between GUI users and non-users (like me). But it did help some friends of mine.

Tony Bove and Cheryl Rhodes had seen their magazine about CP/M, a pre-DOS operating system, fade away. They created a new Mac-centric magazine called *Desktop Publishing* and were back on top again.

The problem was that Apple kept its technology very proprietary. It also kept its prices high. It didn't license the software to anyone else, like IBM, then the biggest maker of PCs. But it lacked the manufacturing capacity to supply the market at lower prices.

So it was that PC software makers led by Microsoft, which had sold IBM its original operating system, PC-DOS, worked frantically for years to match Apple's achievement.

Microsoft and IBM were initially cooperating in this effort, but when Microsoft achieved a key breakthrough, allowing memory over 640K to be addressed by a single program [104] (necessary for a PC GUI

102 The Alto is a good example of how invention is just one piece of the puzzle in creating fortunes. https://en.wikipedia.org/wiki/Xerox_Alto
103 The 49ers won the football game, but more people still talk about the commercial. https://en.wikipedia.org/wiki/1984_(advertisement)
104 A 2017 article describes this "problem." https://www.filfre.net/2017/04/the-640-k-barrier/

to perform its job and remain compatible with MS-DOS), it kept the secret to itself. Microsoft called its GUI Microsoft Windows, and Gates handed me an autographed copy of Version 1.0 at its launch. IBM called its version OS/2.

Thanks to the memory breakthrough, Windows 3.0 was thus the first PC-compatible GUI. Instead of cooperating on a successor, as previously agreed, Microsoft then rolled out a more-powerful version of the same product for servers, Windows NT. OS/2, which IBM thought would take over the world, withered away. [105]

The PC GUI was a big deal. It revolutionized how people used operating systems. But what about networks?

## THE NETWORK GUI

Windows transformed the desktop, wrecking the dreams of IBM, which had dominated computing for over a half century. But what about the network?

Throughout the 1980s, as PC-DOS, the Macintosh, then Windows were being developed, engineers worked the user interface problem. Tim Berners-Lee[106] was one of them, working at CERN, the European Organization for Nuclear Research. He was thinking about using an idea called "hypertext" to link information on different computers.

Berners-Lee didn't invent hypertext. The concept had been around for decades.[107] The term was coined in 1963 by Theodor "Ted" Nelson, whom my wife and I met at the 1984 Comdex show, as Tony Bove and Cheryl Rhodes were closing CP/M.[108]

105 At the height of the battle between Microsoft and IBM, dominated computing. As this was written Microsoft was worth $1.85 trillion, IBM about $135 billion. https://en.wikipedia.org/wiki/OS/2
106 Wikipedia's article on Berners-Lee https://en.wikipedia.org/wiki/Tim_Berners-Lee
107 Wikipedia's article on hypertext. https://en.wikipedia.org/wiki/Hypertext
108 I didn't know it at the time, but Nelson is the son of Hollywood legend Celeste Holm, who starred in "All About Eve" and "High Society," among other films. I learned that at Wikipedia. https://en.wikipedia.org/wiki/Ted_Nelson

Nelson called his proposal for hypertext networking "Project Xanadu" describing it in a book called *Computer Lib/Dream Machines*,[109] which he published back-to-back, the latter upside down, in 1974.

Nelson's idea, however, was grandiose and cumbersome. What Tim Berners-Lee proposed to CERN in 1989 was quick-and-dirty. He combined the Terminal Control Program (TCP) of existing Internet terminals with graphical software running on the NeXT Computer, which Steve Jobs had developed after leaving Apple. He called the resulting software the "World Wide Web" and the name stuck. He was able to create a set of pages on the NeXT within a few months using this Hyper Text Markup Language (HTML) and a simplified version of the authoring software for "browsing" them. The first "web page" describing the new system was put online in 1990.[110]

Work proceeded quickly, moving or "porting" Berners-Lee's solution to other computer systems like those running Microsoft Windows. The breakthrough was NCSA Mosaic browser [111], developed by the National Center for Supercomputing Applications at the University of Illinois in Champaign-Urbana. This browser became widely available in 1993 and I often call 1994 "the year the Web was spun."

It was the combination of a mass market PC GUI, Microsoft Windows, and the successors to the NCSA "web browser" that launched the Internet era.

---

109 I doubt anything but our marriage changed my wife's life so much as finding a copy of Computer Lib/Dream Machines in a Birmingham, AL basement. She went into the basement an accountant, and came out on her way to being a computer programmer. https://en.wikipedia.org/wiki/Computer_Lib/Dream_Machines
110 You can still find this historic Web page at http://info.cern.ch/hypertext/WWW/TheProject.html
111 The University of Illinois team was led by Marc Andreesen, today one of Silicon Valley's leading venture capitalists. https://en.wikipedia.org/wiki/Mosaic_(web_browser)

# Moore's Law of Magnetic Storage

When Gordon Moore was writing his seminal paper, computer data was stored in one of two ways. It was either on tape, or on a disk.

As Jean Hoerni's "planar process" was the key to making microchips possible, An Wang [112] is the father of magnetic memory.

In 1949 Dr. Wang, an immigrant from China, created what he called a "Pulse Transfer Controlling Device," the basic technology for magnetic memory.

Wang's patent, number 2,708,722, granted in 1955, allowed precise control of magnetic energy, replacing cumbersome magnetic drums with spinning metal disks. Wang sold the patent to IBM, which released a five-megabyte memory disk a year later, without mentioning Wang's contribution to it. Wang used the money from IBM to fund his own company, Wang Laboratories. Wang Labs developed one of the early dedicated word processors, one of the first IBM-compatible PCs, and it employed over 30,000 people at its height in 1989.

Wang's memory disk was important because it allowed "random access" – you could grab a piece of data from anywhere on the disk almost immediately. Tape memory, which IBM had introduced in 1952, stored a lot more data, but any music lover of a certain age understands the limitations. If the song you want is at the start of the tape and you're at the end, you must go back through the whole tape to hear the song. The same is true for data stored on tape memory. Still, 2,400-foot tape was the standard in long-term file storage for over 30 years.

The principle of magnetic memory hasn't changed, just as the principle behind making a microprocessor hasn't changed. The magnetic "heads" used to read-and-write data have grown more sensitive. The density with which data can be stored has gone up.

Magnetic memory came in two forms:

---

112    An Wang was one of the great computer entrepreneurs of his time, but it didn't last. https://en.wikipedia.org/wiki/An_Wang

- **Floppy disks**, first sold by IBM in 1967,[113] were portable but offered limited storage. They were defined by their size. The first floppies, released in 1970, were 8-inches in diameter and held 80 Kbytes. The first floppies used on PCs were 5 ¼ inches in diameter and held 180 Kbytes (twice that if you used both sides). The 3 ½ inch, hard-shelled floppy disk introduced in the 1980s could hold 1.44 Mbytes of formatted data. The medium itself is iron oxide, which basically consisted of rust.

- **Hard disks** were first developed in the 1950s [114], but early PC users called these "Winchesters," after a version shipped in 1973 and made from aluminum. Because they were locked inside a case, companies could develop and introduce new hard disk designs freely.

Initially the storage capacity of hard drives seemed to follow Moore's Law. The price-performance of hard drives doubled roughly every 11 months. Then they accelerated.

While the first PC hard drive I bought held 10 Mbytes of data in 1984, 120 Gbyte hard drives were readily available in 2002 for under $300 (that's 12,000 times more data).

By 2009 the largest hard disks were storing 2 Terabytes of data, or 2,000 gigabytes.

In 2019, when I began work on this version of the book, I had a 3 Terabyte hard disk on my desk, for long-term storage, that cost under $200. In 2021, Sandisk was offering 1 Terabyte of memory on a computer chip for under $150.

As hard drive density increased in the 1990s, their makers started running into the same problem chip makers would face a decade later. The distance between magnetic fields was so small that fields were

---

113 In 2021 there's an easy way to tell if you're old. Do you remember floppy disks when they were still floppy? https://en.wikipedia.org/wiki/History_of_the_floppy_disk

114 Wikipedia has a page devoted to the history of hard drives. https://en.wikipedia.org/wiki/History_of_hard_disk_drives

starting to interfere with one another, no matter how carefully they were laid down by a drive's read-write "head."

The solution was found in France, by Albert Fert, and in Germany by Peter Grunberg. Their principle of Giant Magnetoresistance[115] (GMR) brought them the Nobel Prize for Physics in 2007. GMR enabled hard drives to grow in capacity even more rapidly than before.

The concept of GMR is that very weak magnetic changes give rise to big differences in electrical resistance. These differences can also represent fields of data running in many different directions from the read-write head – up, down, sideways, at any number of angles. A read-write head based on this principle reads changes in both magnetic field strength and resistance. These differences in current strength are the 1s and 0s the disk is storing.

The two scientists did their work using very thin layers of material – just a few atoms thick. Both men magnetized one layer up, the other down. A magnetic field was used to run both in the same direction, and the differences in electrical resistance were discovered. Each difference could be read as a separate bit, a 1 or a 0, and when applied to hard drives they delivered exponential improvements in storage capacity, improvements that continue to this day.

While Fert and Grunberg were not working with chips, they were working in an area of materials science which advanced rapidly as new types of chips were engineered. Their work was made possible by the computing progress of Moore's Law, which is why I call this Moore's Law of Magnetic Storage.


## CHIP IT


As I wrote the first two editions of this book, another form of memory came up on the outside, born directly from Moore's Law.

This is chip memory.

---

115    Many inventions made possible or necessary by Moore's Law emerged elsewhere. GMR is just one. https://en.wikipedia.org/wiki/Giant_magnetoresistance

Memory chips have existed for as long as there have been semiconductors. Longer, in fact. The Metal Oxide Semiconductor transistor (MOS) dates from 1959 and was incorporated into chips in 1964. There are many types of memory chip. The point is they're all subject to Moore's Law. The biggest U.S. producer of these chips, Micron Technology, is based on Boise, Idaho because it got crucial early backing from J.R.R. Simplot, the potato magnate. (Chips, get it?)

Memory has been incorporated into microprocessors for decades because it's faster to process from "cache" than to go off-chip for data. Wikipedia has a good history of them. The time it takes to access data from a memory chip is measured in nanoseconds, from disk memory milliseconds. [116]

Chip memory has generally cost more than other types of memory, which is why spinning disks were still common when I wrote the first edition of this book, and optical disks were still common when I wrote the second edition. But as chips have gotten faster, and cheaper, the cost difference has narrowed. The advantages of chips, their smaller size, greater speed, and reliability, have overcome the cost disadvantages. By 2019 chips had replaced other forms of memory in most consumer applications, leaving magnetic semiconductors mainly to clouds, where more permanent storage is desirable and the cost difference becomes meaningful.

## SAVE IT ALL

Applying Moore's Law to memory, both magnetic and semiconductor, now lets us save literally everything.

This has had profound implications. As *American Scientist* magazine noted in 2002 the cost of storing data on disk plunged through the cost of storing it on either paper or film during the 1990s and it continued to go down, approaching $1/10^{th}$ of one cent per megabyte.

---

116 Wikipedia's entry on semiconductor memory. https://en.wikipedia.org/wiki/Semiconductor_memory

The result was a giant conversion of information from paper and film to magnetic media, which not only stores it for nearly nothing but makes it accessible, if the disk where it's stored is connected to a computer that is in turn connected to the Internet.

The Internet, in other words, now gets everything, and keeps it. There's no need to dump old material as data on drives fill up – you just buy new drives. Vast libraries are being compressed onto tiny disks. Those disks are increasingly accessible online.

Old Web pages need never grow old, and never die. They can be cached by Google and stored at sites like the Internet Archive [117]. Web site owners may tell Google not to cache their pages, but when sites die "intestate" (a legal term meaning "without heirs") they may be routinely archived and saved for use by later generations – the cost is that low.

This means the way we think of information is changing, which has profound implications. Nearly everyone is familiar with the format of a book, and the storage problems of books. Our children are more familiar with screens than books, and our grandchildren may see books as mere relics. Screen size, not page size, thus becomes the dominant way to present information.

Nothing is too trivial to save anymore. Web logs and old e-mails are now saved routinely by Internet Service Providers (ISPs). Most messages are saved multiple times, in PCs, by ISPs, and in clouds. Governments are taking advantage and requiring that these logs be made available to law enforcement.

The data we create in our daily lives, when we buy things or even shop, is also saved by companies in vast databases called "data mines." These databases are increasingly being searched by automated programs that seek connections among the data, for commercial purposes. Government conducts such searches for law enforcement purposes as well – whether it can (and the rules under which it can) is a political decision for governments to make. With no worldwide law in place spy agencies are increasingly devoted to what is called "open source

117    The Internet Archive has become one of the most important sites on the network. Most of my own stuff is there or destined to be found only there in time. http://www.archive.org

intelligence," filtering public and private Web pages for connections to adversaries.

The way we think of information is also changing. We no longer think of pages, whether they be Web pages, book pages, or even library indexes. Indexing is done automatically by search engines such as Google, and the main format for all information is becoming the database.

In 2019 many commercial Web sites are becoming databases, with such things as page addresses becoming obsolete. What you saw as the "address" of a "Web page" used to be a straightforward list of subdirectories leading to the page, like this:

http://www.a-clue.com/archive/02/cl020819.htm – The issue of my newsletter, then called a-clue.com, for August 19, 2002.

Now most URLs are dynamic. They're database calls, created in response to user clicks, generated on-the-fly, and often carrying information of how it was reached, like this:

http://www.amazon.com/exec/obidos/subst/home/home.html/002-3806183-1439227 – The Amazon home page, as listed in response to a click made on August 21, 2002.

http://www.amazon.com/exec/obidos/subst/home/home.html/ref%3Dtab%5Fb%5Fgw

%5F1/002-3806183-1439227 – The same Web page address, generated just moments later, in response to a click into a "store" created for my daughter, then back to the home page.

Does this surprise you? It shouldn't.

It has been anticipated for decades, as in the lyrics to "In the Beginning," part of a 1969 Moody Blues album *On the Threshold of a Dream*:

> I've miles
>
> And miles
>
> Of files
>
> Pretty files of your forefather's fruit
>
> and now to suit
>
> our great computer,
>
> You're magnetic ink.

- *In the Beginning* by the Moody Blues [118]

## THE DEATH OF BOOKS

This became clear in 2007 when Amazon.Com brought out the Kindle, a simple computer with a black screen, cheap storage, and broadband Internet capability. By 2009 the Kindle reached Version 2.0, and while it had not replaced books yet, it was already making possible the creation of new kinds of books. Books like this one, with Internet hyperlinks built into them.

By 2019, all the memory on a Kindle was built with chips. Like phones and PCs, there are no longer moving parts on computers, thus nothing to break. Amazon has made it simple to publish books for the Kindle and even order them printed, on-demand. Information is no longer limited to text and pictures, as you are finding if you bought this book in print.

118     The song was written in 1969. You can find the complete lyric here https://genius.com/The-moody-blues-in-the-beginning-lyrics

People still like books, for their feel, and there are still bookstores, just as there are still record stores. But these are designed for nostalgia and serendipity, the joy of finding something interesting completely at random, which is hard to replicate online. They're designed for communication, not for buying books.

Future "books," produced for storage on computer media, will include sound and video as well. The first version of this book, in 2002, was written using footnotes as references, each listed at the bottom of the page, often with Web addresses. The 2010 version was produced exclusively for the Kindle, and the footnotes had become clickable Web addresses. The same with this book, although more of the "links" are to Wikipedia, which doesn't change their addresses the way many other sites do.

Even the notion of "book" is going away. We may well see it as a unit of information no more relevant than the kilometer. A book is an English information mile. I think of a book as a magazine meter, each page a sort of centimeter. But as information moves from paper to the Internet (because it's cheaper to store there) the size of any Web site becomes unlimited.

That's how our children consume media, not as print or sound or video or games, but as a combination of these, to which we can soon add augmented reality where computerized objects are placed in the real world, and virtual reality where completely artificial worlds are presented.

The real unit of media consumption, now, is time. (There's more on the implications of this in Chapter 11, Moore's Law of Content.)

## Moore's Law of Optical Storage

In 1958, just three years after An Wang patented the technology for modern magnetic storage, Bell Labs scientists invented its successor.

The announcement was made in the journal "Physical Review," in an article by

Arthur L. Schawlow, and Charles H. Townes. It was called "Infrared and Optical Masers." [119]

The laser had been born.

The word laser is an acronym for "Light Amplification by Stimulated Emission of Radiation." Light is flashed between two mirrors, one of which (rubies were used first) can be stimulated to emit a beam only at a specific frequency. This "stimulated emission" by the light and mirrors creates a beam of radiation that may be very powerful and go a very long way, but which can also be directed very accurately.

There are many different types of lasers[120] although we're most familiar with the low-power, red beams created by simple ruby lasers. If you aim a modest beam and can read changes in the signal as it bounces back, you have made a bar-code reader. A thin beam can activate a simple switch, as in a TV remote. Or it can place a spot of light on the wall, as in a laser pointer used in a classroom. Laser pointers, originally an important teaching tool, have become cheap enough to be cat's toys and put onto keychains.

On the other hand, if you aim to make a powerful laser beam it may even cut through metal (as with those "ray-guns" you see on TV). There were a wide variety of these machines on the market in 2019. [121]

Lasers also create surgical devices, devices that are easier to control than any knife, knives that heal as they cut. In the 2010s I had laser surgery on the back of one of my eyes to keep the retina from detaching, a condition that cost my mother her sight in the 1970s. One of my sisters, meanwhile, had the more well-known LASIK surgery [122] on the front of her eyeballs, an increasingly common laser surgery technique

119     Bell Labs, then a huge part of the one of America's biggest companies, was proud of its invention. http://www.bell-labs.com/about/history-bell-labs/stories-changed-world/ It is now a small part of the Norwegian company Nokia.
120     Wikipedia offers a history of lasers at https://en.wikipedia.org/wiki/Laser#History
121     Computer-controlled laser cutting is an important ingredient technology in what's called "3-D printing" or "additive manufacturing." https://en.wikipedia.org/wiki/Laser_cutting
122     Wikipedia's entry on LASIK https://en.wikipedia.org/wiki/LASIK

for improving vision by rounding the eyeball.

A variety of lasers are now used for different types of surgery, on everything from feet to teeth to internal organs.[123] Laser surgery suites can cost millions of dollars but enable surgeons to do procedures they couldn't attempt before, efficiently, and safely.

Turning a laser into a storage medium took other breakthroughs. You needed a way to use a laser to read-and-write information. You needed a storage medium. More important, you needed a standard to make the medium portable, as with the floppy disk, and create a mass market.


## Making a CD

The encoding mechanism for laser storage emerged in 1960. This was the same year in which the first working laser was produced.

Since CDs couldn't be written over, like magnetic media, Irving Reed and Gustave Solomon, working at MIT [124], made certain data was correct through what are called "parity bits." A decoder uses these parity bits to correct errors before they're sent to whatever device they are connected to.

Next came the recording medium. Here's how it works.

A laser is focused through a lens placed a fixed distance from the recording medium. The medium is encoded with pits, read as 1s, and landings (or the lack of a pit), recorded as a zero. A second lens, opposite the first, reads the pits and landings onto a photo sensor, which transmits them for translation into data. Motors in the reader move the sensor across the face of the medium (just as in a hard drive) and adjust the speed of the rotating medium, going faster as inside tracks are read, slower as outside tracks are read, so data is always read at the same

123    Wikipedia's entry on laser surgery https://en.wikipedia.org/wiki/Laser_surgery
124    Wikipedia has an entry about Reed-Solomon error correction at https://en.wikipedia.org/wiki/Reed%E2%80%93Solomon_error_correction

speed.

The resulting recording medium can be deceptively simple to make. [125] All you need are a hard substrate a laser can penetrate and a thin film that can encode the pits and landings. An aluminum film is covered in plastic, with some tough acrylic behind it. A label can be placed on the acrylic. The plastic protects the aluminum, which is encoded with pits and lands by a laser with enough power to do that job. It can then be read by a laser with less power. Since we're dealing here with precisely guided light the pits themselves can be very, very tiny. Even in the earliest version of the CD the "recording tracks" were just ½-micron across, one two-millionth of a meter, the space between them a little more than 1 micron.

The third requirement is a standard. A standard is important because the media was designed to be removable, just as a floppy disc can be removed from its drive. Floppy standards focused first on the size of the disk, then on how many sides would contain data, and finally on the density of the recording. The same would be true with optical discs.

Without a standard, discs made by one manufacturer might not play, or might not even fit, in a drive made by another.

The need for standards seems obvious now, but it took nearly two decades for a standard to reach the market. The first Laserdisc patent was granted in 1958 but competing audio formats were still being offered by Sony, Philips, and Matsushita in 1977.

At this point, with the audio CD market looking like it could turn into something, 35 different companies got together in 1978 for what they called the "Digital Audio Disc Convention." A year later Sony and Phillips began working together on what would become the "Red Book"[126] standard for CD-Audio.

The Red Book defines how an audio CD looks and how it works. It defines how many possible tracks a disc can have (99), how many bytes

125     TechTarget still had its article on making optical disks online in 2021.
https://searchstorage.techtarget.com/definition/optical-disc
126     You can still see the Red Book described at https://www.webopedia.com/
TERM/R/Red_Book.html

of data will be in each sector of the disc (3234) and how many bytes in each sector will be used for error correction (392). With all this in hand the way was clear to offer the "revolution" of digital music, with the first music CD, Sony's recording of Billy Joel's *52nd Street*, being released in 1982.

More important, a process had been established, and a recognizable format had been delivered, for portable digital storage with an immense capacity. The original CD-Audio format, which is still in use, holds 70 minutes of music, far more than the LP records it replaced, and with proper care it lasts forever, since the laser doesn't touch it the way a needle reads a record.

That same disk, when simply organized differently (as in the 1983 "Yellow Book") could hold 550 Megabytes of data. A third standard, called the "Green Book," covered CDs containing both software and data, making them interactive. A fourth standard, the "Orange Book," defined a way in which data on a CD could be erased and re-written. All this was done with the same disc, each format backwards compatible with what came before, and all for something you could hold in the palm of your hand.

## MOORE AND LASERS

A fifth CD standard was on its way toward being defined, dubbed a "White Book" for CD-video, when Moore's Law intervened.

By the 1990s engineers had been working for a decade past the delivery of the "Red Book," figuring out new, better ways to put data onto a disk. New lasers were available, using different frequencies of light, and thus it was possible to pack more tracks, and more data, in the same space.

CDs had used an infrared laser. A red light, however, would have a shorter wavelength. This "thinner beam" would mean more pits could be packed on a disc, closer together.

Materials science had also learned to replace a single sheet of aluminum with a more complex material, one with pits in four separate layers. Four layers means four tracks in each location, and four times the capacity on the disc. By bonding the active components of the disc (which are just .6 millimeters (mm) thick) together, you get a "double-sided" disc with even more capacity.

By early in 1995 two separate groups were working on higher-capacity CD discs. Phillips and Sony, developers of the original CD "Red Book" format, were on one side, Time Warner and Toshiba were on the other. For a while it seemed two competing formats might evolve -- remember Beta and VHS videotape? Fortunately, in this case the businessmen remembered their history and peace reigned.

The final standard, called the Digital Video Disk (DVD),[127] was released in December 1995. It represented the best of both worlds. From Sony and Phillips came the idea of compatibility between CDs and DVDs. From Toshiba and Time Warner came the idea of the double-sided disk, and the possibility (from 3M) of having multiple layers on a single disc.

Technically, there are four different DVD capacities although as with CDs any DVD player would be backward-compatible with formats that came out before it was made:

4.7 GB (Single Layer Single Side)

8.5 GB (Dual Layer Single Side)

9.4 GB (Single Layer Double Side)

17.0 GB (Dual Layer Double Side)

Instead of considering this as data capacity, think of it as video capacity. (That's what the "White Book" was all about, remember – a video CD.) Even a single layer, single sided DVD could contain 133 minutes of full motion high-quality digital video. And you don't have to "turn-over" the double-sided disc, either – a DVD player can switch sides seamlessly.

---

127      Wikipedia's DVD article https://en.wikipedia.org/wiki/DVD

In practice manufacturers ramped-up this capacity more slowly than they did with CDs. Instead of building high-end devices and letting their prices fall the way computers do, the consumer electronics companies behind the DVD standards wanted a fixed price, with increasing capacity over time.

Still, all the capacities seen with CDs are there with the DVD. There's a standard for storing data (as opposed to video) on DVDs, a separate standard for audio, and a standard for DVDs you can encode or "burn" yourself.

By 2002 the DVD had taken off. DVD players were available for under $100. Video rental chains like *Blockbuster Video* began to emphasize the rental of discs, rather than videotapes. Computers no longer came with floppy disk drives, but players that could write CDs and play DVDs.

Of course, this wasn't the end of the story.

Smaller tracks meant more capacity, and two new formats delivered them during the first decade of the 2000s – BluRay and HD-DVD. It was expected these would be perfect for High Definition TV (HDTV) recordings, which began in 2009 with the switch to digital transmission. Instead of waging this fight in standards bodies, however, it was waged in the market, HD-DVD being abandoned in 2008.

But as great as DVDs delivered to your door, or costing just $10 each, might be, Moore's Law was about to make them obsolete as this book was being revised in 2010. By 2019 it would be ancient history

## Moore's Law of Optical Fiber

In 30 years, storage had moved from floppy disks carrying words to BluRay discs storing high-definition movies, from hard drives holding megabytes to cheap hard drives holding terabytes. How was all this data to move online?

The answer lies in combining the silicon used in most semiconductors with light traveling through lasers.

This is optical fiber. Optical fiber is one of the 20th century's great inventions. I put it right up there with the microchip.

You can learn a lot more about optical fiber and its history from Jeff Hecht in his book *City of Light*. [128]

Glass has been drawn into fiber since the days of the Roman Empire. It was woven into cloth as early as 1873. Its most popular early use, of course, was as fiberglass, which has been around since the 1930s.

But the real breakthroughs came after 1960, when laser technology was in its infancy. Almost immediately, researchers began looking at optical fiber as a transmission medium for laser light. The field of optoelectronics – combining light with electronics – was born.

It's a field distinct from microprocessors, with its own technical jargon. It's also a field of engineering with wide application in everything from barcode scanners and CD players to flat-screen TVs.

By 1970 Corning Glass had developed a way to combine fibers and lasers so they could transmit light at long distances with minimal loss. By 1976 Bell Labs was testing a fiber optic system that could transmit 45 megabits of data per second, with minimal loss. This work was done at a plant in Norcross, Georgia, a suburb of Atlanta.

I was able to tour this plant soon after moving to Atlanta in 1982, when it was still owned by AT&T. (It is now owned by OFS, a Japanese company.) It was an amazing experience. Tubes of very pure glass were hung at the top of a structure, heated very carefully, then slowly pulled like taffy. Miles and miles of fiber would emerge, over time, from a single tube. The fiber was quickly coated in plastic, then bundled with other fibers into a wire coated with heavier plastic, then shipped.

Back in the early 80s, splicing the cable so that fibers lined up precisely remained a problem, but the executives who led my tour were confident good, cheap solutions were just around the corner. They were

128    Here is how you can buy City of Light right now, from Amazon.Com
https://www.amazon.com/exec/obidos/ASIN/0195108183

right.

Their great ambition then was to transform the telephone network from a copper plant running calls as analog signals into a fiber plant that transmitted calls (and data) digitally. The revolution would be expensive, it would require digging up streets and rewiring poles, but over the next 20 years that's just what happened.


## How Does Optical Fiber Work?

Like all great inventions optical fiber is simple in concept.

An optical fiber isn't pure glass. That plastic they wrap it in is a reflective material that acts as a mirror. A "transmitter" (a diode emitting laser light) sends light into the fiber, modulating it on-and-off to represent 1s (light on) or 0s (light off).

The light bounces off the walls of the tube, following the glass as the path of least resistance. At the other end of the line a "photo detector" reads the light. If the light is on it reads a 1, if off it reads a 0. In a long line there may be a "regenerator" installed to keep the signal boosted – it reads the low power signal and sends it along as a stronger signal. Amplifiers can eliminate the need for regeneration.

The word "light" here was something of a misnomer. The light read by the earliest photo detectors was at low frequencies, which attenuated (died away) slowly. This was infrared light that can't, in fact, be seen with the naked eye.

Like the earliest computer microchips, glass (and thus fiber) is primarily made with silicon. The silica comes from sand. Other chemicals are added by the glass maker, such as flux to lower the melting temperature, and stabilizers to make the glass stronger. While the base material is simple, the recipes for various types of glass vary, with such metals as aluminum, lead, boron, magnesium, and iron all used to various degrees and for various purposes.

The difference between fiber and a computer chip is in what makes them work. While the microprocessor is pushing electrons, fiber is pushing photons. The trick in building networks of fiber, then, is translating between electricity and light. This is done through what are called electro-optical devices.

## BELL LABS DISCOVERS COLORS

By the 1990s the telephone industry's transition from analog to digital was well underway, and fiber was at the center of it. Copper long-distance lines were being replaced wholesale by fiber cables, and telephone industry giants were vying to run long distance cables under the oceans.

The math seemed simple enough. If one fiber could handle 45 Mbps of data, then you could easily bundle 100 of them together and run 4,500 Mbps of data. Of course, you wouldn't need to run all of this at once. You'd want extra strands for redundancy (in case some broke), and you'd want each line to have extra capacity for growth. You might also increase the capacity of a line slightly, by shortening the time between light pulses.

But Moore's Law was about to change the game again. Using colors.

The technical term is Wavelength Division Muliplexing[129] As any kid who has seen a sun shower knows, light isn't just white. It comes in colors, a rainbow of colors. The principle behind seeing the colors is called diffraction. Different colors can be diffracted out of white light, and each color has its own wavelength.

To create the rainbow principle in an optical fiber you need to separate, or multiplex, the various wavelengths. This was first done through "gratings," cutting the fiber in such a way that different wavelengths would be diffracted in slightly different directions. Once diffraction was proven, and diffracted waves could be created and read separately, progress came very rapidly. A scientist interviewed in 1997 talked about

---

129     Wikipedia has an article on Wide Division Multiplexing https://
en.wikipedia.org/wiki/Wavelength-division_multiplexing

"tens" of different channels. In 1999 Bell Labs demonstrated a system with over 1,000 different channels.

That's a lot of colors.

## Colors in Motion

Each advance in lasers and multiplexing was followed by products implementing the new standards.

The result was huge jumps in the capacity of fiber lines, far more than that predicted by Moore's Law. (Remember that Moore's Law was written to apply to microprocessors, not optical fiber.)

The first fiber cable to cross an ocean, TAT-8, went into service in 1988 with a capacity of 280 Mbps. Just 10 years cables were being planned whose capacity was measured in terabits, 1,000 gigabits, or 1 million megabits. On one cable.

Getting from those slow speeds to higher ones could increase the capacity of a line by a factor of 10 or 100. Equipment suppliers were able to easily sell billions of dollars in upgrade gear for use in long distance lines and metropolitan networks. Networks were upgraded without the cable being replaced.

Despite the increases in capacity for individual cables, new cables were being laid constantly. On the great oceanic routes demand was growing at 150% per year during the late 1990s. Investors saw the growth of Internet usage, especially in Asia, and the promise of broadband increasing an individual's bandwidth demand by a factor of 20 at a stroke, and poured money into WDM technology, cabling, and construction.

I witnessed this on the streets of Atlanta during the dot-com heyday of the 1990s. The U.S. government was encouraging the growth of fiber cabling, and regulations prevented cities from doing much more than watch private interests work once they had the right-of-way. Railroads and electricity companies couldn't deny fiber cables that right-of-way either (although they could charge for it). Since my home was close to both a railroad line and high-capacity electric lines, the roads became packed with metal plates, used at night to disguise holes where workers were laying cable. Some stayed on the ground for months.


## Enron and the Kitten Market


Near the height of the dot com boom a Houston company called Enron was playing fast-and loose with technology, markets, and the law.

But it would soon be destroyed by Moore's Law.

Enron was launched in the 1980s as an energy company. I knew its predecessor firm as Houston Natural Gas, a staid gas utility. In the 1990s, instead of remaining a utility, Enron began making markets in energy. It bought, sold, and traded gas, oil, and electricity the way Wall Street firms traded pork belly futures. Not only did it organize the markets, but it was a participant in those markets, earning the kind of profits a dealer with a knowledge of fancy shuffles can earn at a poker table. Allegedly it played all sorts of other games to hide profits (and losses) from its shareholders, moving money into offshore affiliates and debt instruments.

The Internet was Enron's great tool. The Internet allowed its traders to stay in touch with the markets, with one another, and with other traders. Enron's culture seemed to be like that of Microsoft, where the smartest people with the "highest bandwidth" (Microsoft-speak for smarts) were given free rein. In developing this culture Enron was following the advice of its own consultants, McKinsey & Co.

Enron was politically plugged-in (its executives advised Gov. George W. Bush and his Presidential campaign, while also giving substantially to Democrats), its results always seemed to "beat the market," and its stock price kept rising through the bubble years.

It was in 1999 that Enron made a fatal mistake. It decided to enter the market for long distance fiber bandwidth. The company began signing contracts for using the fiber in its own network.

92

But bandwidth isn't like oil, or gas, or electricity. Thanks to WDM, it's like kittens.

Let me explain that.

In the energy markets, you have a good idea of supply as well as demand. (I started my journalism career in Houston, covering the oil boom of the late 1970s.) Someone in the "oil patch" might bring in a new field, or a utility might adjust its generating capacity in response to summer's demand for air conditioning. But a savvy trader can balance supply-and-demand, on a yearly, monthly, even real-time basis. Plus, if you're both running the market and playing in it, you're like a Vegas card dealer who knows some card tricks and is betting in their own game – you can't lose.

But bandwidth doesn't work that way. Bandwidth supply can explode, exponentially, and suddenly, thanks to Moore's Law of Optical Fiber. A company has one fiber line, but changes the electronics at each end, and suddenly it has 100 or 1,000 times as much bandwidth as before. Or a company is using a half-dozen fibers in one line and then decides to turn on or "light" hundreds of other fibers in the same cable, again exploding capacity. (When a company puts a fiber line into production it is said to "light" the line. When it takes a line out of production that line goes "dark" and becomes "dark fiber.")

My analogy is to kittens.

Economics teachers like to talk about widgets in their classes – imaginary products with endless utility but no real economic value. Kittens are the same way. They're great, but unless you can limit supply with purebreds, they have absolutely zero economic value.

Enron found itself trading kittens. It signed a contract for bandwidth, then assumed all its lines would sell for the same price. It knew the bandwidth was really costing it nothing to produce, so it set aside all the incoming revenue as profit.

Here's the problem.

Mr. & Mrs. Enron have two cats and a litter of 8 kittens. Some fool offers them $100 for one of the kittens. They take the money, call it profit, and look again at the litter. I guess that means we have $700 worth of kittens, they figure, plus we still have the cats. Those cats might produce, say, a half-dozen more litters over their lifetime. And the kittens will produce cats, too. The "asset value" of the two cats may now be as much as $10,000. Guess where they put the money. They bought more cats.

But anyone whose cat has ever gotten pregnant knows that's not right. Yes, some fool might buy one of your kittens. Generally, kittens are hard to even give away. It's a relief for most families to relieve themselves of litters, and the next thing most families do is take those cats to the vet to get fixed, so the nightmare won't return

Enron's oh-so-clever "bandwidth traders" didn't know they were selling kittens. They thought they were selling an asset like oil or gas, something whose supply was limited amid growing demand. In fact they were selling something whose demand was growing arithmetically but whose supply was growing geometrically, in line with Moore's Law of Optical Fiber.

A lot of other companies made the same mistake. In fact, the whole energy sector was treating bandwidth as an energy market. But when reality hit, when "last-mile" demand didn't meet the unlimited supply made possible by WDM and Moore's Law, Enron was caught out.

In 2001, executives seriously debated whether the "bandwidth glut" was fact or fiction. Reality eventually hit. It was fact. So-called "OC-3" circuits, 155 Mbps lines running between New York and Los Angeles, worth $1.8 million per year in 2000, were trading for under $150,000 just 16 months later.


## THE TELECOM COLLAPSE

The same factors that caught Enron also caught 2002's other great bankrupt, Worldcom.

Worldcom wasn't a trading company. It was what stock experts call a "roll-up," acquiring all the players in the market with the hope of then making monopoly profits.

For 15 years chairman Bernie Ebbers bought larger long-distance companies, mostly for stock, accumulating market share and assets. He started in the 1980s, when the telephone industry was still mostly analog. He knew the industry would move toward digital technology but figured that, if he held the bulk of the market, his market power would allow him to keep prices high even in the face of falling costs.

In 1997 Worldcom bought MCI, the second-largest long-distance carrier in the U.S. In 1999 it tried to buy Sprint, the third-largest carrier, but regulators saw the game it was playing and said no. Along the way Worldcom also bought most what was then the Internet's broadband capacity.

In many industries a "roll-up" is a sound strategy. AT&T and Verizon control most of the mobile market and gain huge profits as a result. It's a shared monopoly, in this case a duopoly. With supply in a small number of hands by 1999, many analysts figured this was happening in the telecommunications business.

But demand for service doesn't mean money in a carrier's pocket. A software-based technology called Voice over IP (VOIP) let voice calls route over the Internet, bypassing phone networks and letting vendors advertise "free long distance." By 2009, while on a visit to China, I was able to use the technology, in the form of Google Talk, to speak to my wife "free".

Worldcom's "dominance" of the Internet long distance market or "core" also proved to be a chimera. How can you have "market control" when any market participant can quickly increase their own carrying capacity infinitely? What happens in that case is that prices fall toward zero. Prices can even fall below costs. Worldcom tried to cover up this new reality with accrual accounting, counting income before it was realized, [130] but went bankrupt in 2002. [131] CEO Ebbers was sentenced

130     *The Balance* described this magic trick https://www.thebalance.com/worldcom-s-magic-trick-356121
131     Fortune Magazine described the bankruptcy filing as the largest in history

to a 25-year jail term in 2005. He died in 2020, one month after being released from prison on compassionate grounds.[132]

## Moore's Law of Networking

The dynamics of Moore's Law do not just apply to microprocessors, although that was all Moore wrote about.

The rules also apply, albeit in different ways, for all a computer's inputs-and-outputs, for storage and networks. Research that is applied in one profitable direction can be applied in others with huge results. The impact of all this is multiplied when one system, like the Internet, can take advantage of progress in several areas – processing, storage, and optoelectronics.

Once an industry moves entirely from analog to digital technology, as was happening in telecommunications by 2002, a new kind of economics takes hold. When the costs of market inputs are dropping, supply can go up exponentially. The bigger the industry where this takes place, the more dramatic the result.

Moore's Law and the Internet aren't directly related, but they do reinforce one another. Not only did advances in microelectronics (and storage) advance the state of the art in optics, but the Internet sped these advances to the market.

The same thing that happened with magnetic storage has now happened with optical storage and fiber optic cables. Supply growth can outpace that of demand, resulting in lower prices.

When Moore's Law hit the telecommunications market, the results were catastrophic – for the carriers. Once the carriers went bust, so did many of the industry's suppliers. Many people who had spent their working lives in optoelectronics suddenly found themselves out of

---

to that time. http://archive.fortune.com/galleries/2009/fortune/0905/gallery.largest_bankruptcies.fortune/3.html

132      Wikipedia has a complete description of Ebbers' story https://en.wikipedia.org/wiki/Bernard_Ebbers

work. But anyone familiar with the engineering involved could have predicted these results – fools and their money are soon parted.

The winners here are you and me.

# CHAPTER 6

# MOORE'S LAW OF RADIOS

Moore's Law applies not just to chips but to everything computer chips touch. It applies to storage and to optical fiber for moving data. But it also applies to radios, and this may be the most important impact it has on your daily life.

Thanks to Moore's Law we're living in the Golden Age of Radio.

## THE GOLDEN AGE OF RADIO?

The first radio was a data set.

Whether you believe Guglielmo Marconi[133] or Nikola Tesla[134] was behind it, the fact is that the first radio sets transmitted and received digital data, not analog waves, in the form of the dots-and-dashes of Morse Code, originally been crafted for the telegraph. [135]Marconi's company sold these devices to ships like the Titanic, and the "S.O.S." distress call became a movie cliché.

Marconi's patents were recognized by the British government and resulted in a British company called Marconi. It merged with other English companies[136] and its name survived until 2005, when it was bought by Swedish international L.M. Ericsson[137], which spun-out some

133     Marconi was born in France, but his mother was Irish and he made his name in England. https://en.wikipedia.org/wiki/Guglielmo_Marconi
134     Nikola Tesla made many things in his life. Cars weren't among them. https://en.wikipedia.org/wiki/Invention_of_radio#Tesla's_boat
135     This might be a good time for me to recommend Tom Standage's great book *The Victorian Internet*, a history of the telegraph. Available at Amazon. https://www.amazon.com/dp/B07JW5WQSR/
136     Wikipedia on Marconi Communications https://en.wikipedia.org/wiki/Marconi_Communications
137     Ericsson was a bigger name in the history of electricity than Marconi. https://www.infoworld.com/article/2673163/ericsson-to-buy-most-of-marconi-for--2-1b.html

of the assets under the name Telent. Telent[138], privately held in 2021, was still providing networking services in Europe.

The first analog radio broadcast occurred in 1906[139], Marconi opened his first radio factory in 1912, and the first radio broadcasters began transmission in 1920. But analog broadcaster signals quickly began interfering with one another, resulting in a regulatory regime under the Radio Act of 1927[140], creating a Federal Radio Commission that was made part of the Federal Communications Commission in the next decade.

The point is that while we think of "radio" as a simple, even old-fashioned, analog technology, mainly used for broadcasting entertainment, it has always been a digital technology, used for sending messages from point-to-point. Progress in transmitting data over the air has been going on for well over a century.

## THE MOTHER OF DIGITAL RADIO

Hedy Lamarr was a Hollywood actress famous for the aphorism, "Any girl can be glamorous. All you have to do is stand there and look stupid,"[141], as quoted in a 1962 book by reviewer Richard Schickel called "The Stars."

But as Hedwig Kiesler (1914-2000)[142], born in Vienna as the First World War was beginning, was not stupid. A self-taught inventor, she worked on things like improved traffic lights and a tablet that created a carbonated beverage which she said, "tasted like Alka-Seltzer."

Lamarr's most famous invention was unknown to the public for

---

138     Telent is focused on the public safety radio niche https://telent.com/
139     Wikipedia offers a complete history of radio. https://en.wikipedia.org/wiki/History_of_radio
140     Wikipedia has a separate page on the Radio Act, as it was called.  https://en.wikipedia.org/wiki/Radio_Act_of_1927
141     Needless to say my favorite Lamarr quote. https://en.wikiquote.org/wiki/Hedy_Lamarr
142     Hedy Lamarr had been virtually forgotten when I wrote the first edition of this book. Now she is a legend again, as she should be. https://en.wikipedia.org/wiki/Hedy_Lamarr

over 50 years. This was a system for avoiding German jamming of radio signals, created with avant-garde composer George Antheil in 1942. Her first husband, Fritz Mandel, had become a Nazi arms supplier after they separated, and Hedy Lamarr spent much of World War II entertaining Allied troops. For Hedwig Kiesler, the war was personal.

Her idea, based on how Antheil coordinated player pianos for his "Ballet Meanique," was that if the notes represented radio frequencies, and both ends of a conversation switched among them in time to the "music," the switches would seem random, and the transmission would be undetectable. Because there were 88 keys on a piano, the system used 88 frequencies.

Military secrecy buried Lamarr's invention. It wasn't until 1957, with the patent about to expire, that Sylvania researchers took up her idea, using electronics instead of piano rolls for the frequency hopping. Their systems worked for the purpose Lamarr intended, securing communication from eavesdropping. They were used during the Cuban Missile Crisis of 1962. Still, the patent remained classified for over 20 years after its expiration.

After newspaper and magazine reporters re-discovered Lamarr's role in what had become known as "frequency hopping," in the late 1980s, she became increasingly celebrated. This culminated in 1997 when she and Antheil were given the "Pioneer Award"[143] by the Electronic Frontier Foundation. (Antheil's award was posthumous.)

After Lamarr's death in 2000, her fame only grew. She was the subject of the 2018 documentary *Bombshell*,[144] Actress Gal Gadot (best known for *Wonder Woman*) signed to play Lamarr in 2018, for a Showtime mini-series based on her life.[145] That project had still not gone before the cameras as this was being written. [146]

---

143    I was working for a magazine called Boardwatch back then and was very happy to see her celebrated during her lifetime. https://en.wikipedia.org/wiki/EFF_ Pioneer_Award

144    The listing on IMDB https://www.imdb.com/title/tt6752848/

145    The AV Club had the story. https://news.avclub.com/gal-gadot-wants-to-produce-star-in-a-hedy-lamarr-serie-1828146600

146    This was still true in early 2021. https://www.ibtimes.com/gal-gadot-goes-hiking-daughter-photos-2754524

Lamarr's story is also told in Richard Rhodes' book *Hedy's Folly* and in the children's book *Hedy Lamarr's Double Life*.[147] Young girls in 2019 celebrate her in their school reports and as a role model combining beauty, brains, and patriotism.

Here's a piece of trivia. Look at Lamarr's filmography[148] for the years in question, roughly from 1940-1942. In films like *Boom Town*, *Tortilla Flat*, *Ziegfeld Girl* and *H.M Putnam Esq*, she consistently played brainy women, often with careers, always with a sense of humor. These women carried the moral center of the picture, even in supporting roles. After her war work was finished, Lamarr was returned to playing dumb, femme fatale roles. Small wonder she became cynical about the movie business.

For Hedy Lamarr's invention to change the world, as with GUIs, Moore's Law needed to create some enabling technology.

## Texas Makes Hedy's Invention Beautiful

Lamarr's breakthrough would still be irrelevant today except for a specific type of silicon chip called a Digital Signal Processor (DSP)[149] or digital encoder.

As the name implies, a DSP translates analog information that comes into as a discrete series of numbers. All you then need is a device that measures something and turns it into digital information, and you have a market for a DSP. Texas Instruments remains the leading maker of DSP chips and systems.

DSPs are used in all sorts of everyday products, everything from audio and video systems to cars and power tools. DSPs power your digital camera and printer. The military uses them to guide missiles, and

---

147    *Hedy's Double Life* is available on Amazon.Com https://www.amazon.com/Hedy-Lamarrs-Double-Life-Hollywood/dp/1454926910
148    Hedy Lamarr's complete filmography https://www.imdb.com/name/nm0001443/
149    DSPs are commonly called encoders https://en.wikipedia.org/wiki/Digital_signal_processor

they're at the heart of most fiber communications systems. Anything that can be digitized in any way can be analyzed and transformed by a DSP.

But it all began with a toy. If you're of a certain age you probably remember it.

It was called the *Speak and Spell* [150]and it was one of the most important toys ever made, so important there's one in The Smithsonian Institution. Kids would spin a wheel and a DSP would "speak" the letter it stopped at.

As Intel grew to dominate the market for microprocessors in the 1980s, thanks to the IBM PC and PC "clones," Texas Instruments focused on DSP technology, becoming the dominant player in the encoder market. In this way both inventors of integrated chip technology came up big winners – Robert Noyce, with Intel in microprocessors, Jack Kilby of Texas Instruments in DSPs.

## How DSPs Work

DSPs are based on a concept called "saturation arithmetic"[151].

The idea is to combine math and time. Each tick of the clock creates a new measurement, the original field having been "saturated." The faster the clock, the more accurate the reproduction of the signal. Each point in time measures a level, each level is saved. This lets a digital system mimic an analog input, much as calculus is used to measure a curve. A DSP can analyze and report on any analog input.

The application of saturation arithmetic to DSPs resulted in a real-time DSP patent. It was credited to a Frenchman, Giuseppe DiGuigno[152], and assigned to a French institute. This transformed

---

150    The Speak & Spell may have been the most groundbreaking toy ever invented. https://en.wikipedia.org/wiki/Speak_%26_Spell_(toy)

151    Wikipedia has a good explanation at https://en.wikipedia.org/wiki/Saturation_arithmetic

152    Google has the patent listing https://patents.google.com/patent/EP0104290B1/en

the chip market as few events have since the invention of the microprocessor.

Once a computer could use analog data in real-time, the way was open to put computers inside any device that gathered analog data, like sound or pictures, and the results could be displayed in a digital format. TI saw this coming and decided that, rather than fighting Intel in the microprocessor market, it invested in DSPs and dominated the new market.

The impact of this is often underestimated because many companies making systems that use DSPs don't call them DSPs. TI is so closely associated with the DSP acronym that the other players look like minnows. Thus, many DSP chips go to market as "encoders," like those that translate video streams under the MPEG standard.

The market for programmable DSP chips was estimated in 2002 to be worth over $4 billion. By 2008 the market was estimated to be worth $7.8 billion. It is expected to reach $19.5 billion by 2025. [153]

What does this have to do with Moore's Law of Radios?

In a data radio system, the DSP is the crucial interface between the radio frequency signal and everything a computer might do with the signal, the key translation point. Since DSPs are chips, they can improve the translation at a rate consistent with Moore's Law.

## SPREAD SPECTRUM

While Lamarr and Antheil focused on protecting against eavesdropping, they also created a way to use radio frequencies efficiently. Signals could move among frequency bands in reaction to interference. Signals could use a new frequency while still using the old one.

The concept, now called "spread spectrum" technology, was first implemented for civilian use as part of the Global Positioning Satellite (GPS) system in the 1970s, used to help people measure their location

153    https://www.marketwatch.com/press-release/digital-signal-processors-dsp-market-size-to-grow-at-93-cagr-to-hit-usd-19500-million-by-2025-2019-06-04

on the Earth with great precision. It was first used commercially by a company called Equatorial Communications Inc. for synchronizing signals from its satellites.[154]

Spread spectrum sounds complicated but is easy to comprehend once you understand the original invention. The signal that seeks out other receivers, called the carrier wave, uses a wider piece of spectrum than the data encoded within it. The wave changes frequency in a seemingly random pattern, and this pattern is picked up by a receiver. The receiver picks up the carrier, then picks up the data inside it, then goes looking for another carrier.

By hopping among frequencies in this way, "spread spectrum" doesn't just resist jamming or detection by a receiver that isn't attuned to it. It also makes sure that the available frequencies are used efficiently, because when one slice of spectrum is blocked the radio goes to another frequency. (The overlapping carrier waves don't contain data, and they're ignored by other devices sharing the spectrum.) When a lot of radios are using the same piece of spectrum, in other words, "spread spectrum[155]" assures that the signals can avoid interference on their own, without human intervention.

Qualcomm Inc. of San Diego brought spread spectrum technology to the mass market in the form of Code Division Multiple Access (CDMA), a system for efficient use of spectrum by cellphones, starting in the mid-1980s. CDMA applied the lessons of the Lamarr patent to the problem of cellular spectrum scarcity.

From the beginning, cellular telephony was dependent on computers. The idea was that instead of blasting signals from a single, central antenna tower, smaller towers requiring less power would be spread around a city. By using less power, spectrum could be re-used and the receivers, too, could operate with less power. When one cell tower was regularly filled with calls its service area, too, could be split, creating more "cells," and re-using the same frequency yet-again. Computers coordinated everything and, as they improved, so did the coordination

154    Here is Wikipedia's page on GPS and its history https://en.wikipedia.org/wiki/Global_Positioning_System
155    Here is Wikipedia's page on spread spectrum https://en.wikipedia.org/wiki/Spread_spectrum

and efficiency.

By encoding voices digitally, using DSPs and spread spectrum technology, a clear voice call could be sent using less radio bandwidth than was possible with an analog call. By sending out calls digitally instead of using regular radio signals, moreover, they couldn't be heard by a scanner – they were protected from eavesdroppers.

In 2019 Qualcomm, which has continually improved its system and made communications chips based on it, was the dominant supplier of cellular modems. It had the power to link purchase of its modems to licensing of its patents. Despite international efforts to break the monopoly, it was still holding as this was written. [156]

The combination of saturation arithmetic, DSPs, and Hedy Lamarr's invention were the ingredients necessary to apply Moore's Law to digital radios.

## MOORE'S LAW AND SPREAD SPECTRUM

While spread spectrum is easy to explain, it's complex to implement.

This is where Moore's Law comes into play. As chips got faster, they improved the efficiency of the cellular network and the phones that accessed them. Thanks to Moore's Law, cellular phones (and systems) got cheaper, better, and more efficient all at the same time. By creating a problem for computers to solve in frequency hopping, cellular telephony brought the benefits of Moore's Law into radios.

Writing a book about technology in 2002, revising it in 2010 and revising it again 10 years later shows how fast Moore's Law works.

» **In 2002,** cell phones were just becoming ubiquitous, and Nokia "candy bar" phones were state of the art. We had one, and a wired phone at home, so when our son ran off chasing our dogs (don't ask) one of us drove around town looking for him while

---

156    Even Apple lost to Qualcomm, as *Tom's Guide* reported. https://www. tomsguide.com/us/qualcomm-vs-apple-patent-case,news-29649.html

the other sat at home and waited for a call.' A lot of people saw Short Message Services (SMS), 140-character notes sent between cellphones, as state of the art.

» **By 2010**, the Apple iPhone was a new thing. I had immediately seen it for what it was, an "Internet terminal," a computer you could hold in your hand. Many people were buying iPhones or looking forward to getting competing phones using Google's Android system, introduced in 2008. Many people were starting to combine SMSs into Mobile Message Services (MMS), to send longer messages containing pictures between phones.

» **In 2019** smartphones were ubiquitous. Smartphones had become the primary computer for most people around the world. We no longer thought much of SMS or MMS, technologies based on telephony, preferring Internet services hosted in clouds like those of Apple and Google. What had been home theater or desktop applications, like Netflix, had also moved to the phone.

» **By 2021** even Twitter, whose short message lengths were based on the SMS standard, had abandoned it, allowing in-line videos with tweets.


Not all cellular advances are visible. The same forces making phones smaller, cheaper, lighter, and more capable also impact cellular phone "base stations" those phones connect with. Those stations, too, are becoming more efficient, less costly, smaller, and their electricity requirements are going down. By 2019 carriers like Sprint had begun deploying base stations that fit on utility poles or on the sides of buildings, rather than requiring tall cell towers. With the launch of 5G services in 2021, this will likely become ubiquitous, since 5G brings much-shorter wavelengths, which attenuate over very short distances, into the Internet mainstream.

# OPEN SOURCE FOR RADIOS

Smartphones use frequency bands that have been sold by government to carriers. But not all calls are metered because in the 1980s the government did something good.

By the late 1980s the FCC was getting all kinds of proposals for new and novel uses of the frequency spectrum. Rather than write specific rules and authorizations for each new technology and each new piece of equipment, it created the "Part 15" rules. [157]

Under Part 15, the license to use the spectrum is held by the device, not its operator. It's as though you were licensing the radio rather than the station. Instead of selling carriers specific frequency bands, the Part 15 rules let anyone create, build, sell and use a product within designated parts of the frequency spectrum without having a license to own that spectrum. With "Part 15" the FCC, for the first time, authorized unlicensed uses of FCC spectrum.

The initial beneficiaries were low power radio stations serving small towns or college campuses. The Part 15 rules allowed them to operate without government interference. But other types of devices quickly began appearing to use this "unlicensed" spectrum. Garage-door openers, for instance, operate under "Part 15" rules. Cordless phones, like the one I used in the 1990s, operated under "Part 15" rules as well.

As engineers learned to make use of higher frequency ranges through the 1980s and 1990s, the FCC and Part 15 followed, creating more "unlicensed" bands. There's a Part 15 band between 425-435 MHz, mainly used by "ham" radio enthusiasts. There are Part 15 bands as low as 43 MHz and as high as 77 GHz.

For most of the 1990s the most important Part 15 bands were those around 900 MHz, 2.4 GHz, and 5.3-5.8 GHz. [158]

---

157    The Part 15 rules are explained at https://www.vpilaboratories.com/services_fcc_part_15.php

158    These are frequently referred to now as the "WiFi bands," although more recent FCC rulemaking will add to them. https://en.wikipedia.org/wiki/ISM_band

A.  The spectrum between 902-928 MHz is still most often associated with Industrial, Medical, and Scientific (ISM) uses. This is the frequency range that was used by cordless telephones. They're also used by wireless sensors and Radio Frequency Identification (RFID) inventory tags.

B.  B.  The frequency between 2.4-2.4835 GHz, is today better known as the lower Wireless Fidelity or WiFi. The channels are wide, because the frequency is high (thus the waves are shorter than at 900 MHz) and the distances they can travel in a circle are just a few hundred feet.

C.  C.  The third set of frequency ranges, originally called the U-NII (Unlicensed National Information Infrastructure) bands, when they were licensed in 1997, were created for home networking applications and is known as the upper WiFi band. There are 350 MHz of frequency – 200 MHz in two bands one between 5.150-5.350 GHz and another between 5.725-5.875 GHz. Again, shorter wavelengths mean shorter waves covering less area. But 350 MHz – 350 million hertz -- is enough frequency in which to move 350 million bits of data each second, without compressing the signal, far more than what's required for a high definition movie.

Frequencies assigned to "Part 15" use can deliver any radio service – voice, video, or data. So long as they don't interfere with other users, they can deliver this service anywhere, even in your home. You can use them for a Local Area Network as easily as you can a cordless phone or garage door opener. Just buy a router and hook your broadband modem to it.

## THE BIRTH OF WIFI

The first wireless data network was built long before Part 15. It was in 1971, in Hawaii, and was known as ALOHAnet[159]. Seven computers on four islands were arranged in a star-like formation and were able to

---

159     AlohaNet didn't last long but it was an important experiment. https://en.wikipedia.org/wiki/ALOHAnet

communicate data without wires.

What we call WiFi was born after the Institute of Electrical and Electronics Engineers (IEEE or I-triple E) created a working group to study the Part 15 regulations under the FCC's Rule 802.11. This became known as the "802.11" working group[160].

It took the group seven years to come up with a standard, running data at a maximum rate of 1-2 Mbps. That wasn't very fast, so the committee went right back to work.

By 1999 it had plans for two new standards:

- 802.11a would work within the new U-NII bands and provide a maximum speed of 54 Mbps.
- 802.11b would work within the older 2.4 GHz band and provide a maximum speed of 11 Mbps.

There are many ways to use a frequency band, depending on how much power you apply toward creating waves on it that hold data. In the 2.4 MHz band, for instance, the 802.11 working group saw separate applications depending on how much power was applied toward creating the wave – low, medium, or high:

- Bluetooth would require very little power, only work between two points at once, and is now frequently used for wireless headsets, keyboards, and other peripherals. It runs at only 761 Kbps.

- Local Area Networks were what we generally think of when we think of WiFi. When I first decided to network my kids' computers, in the late 1990s, I ran Ethernet networking cable under the floorboards. The 802.11 standards made this obsolete.

- Point-to-point links, using the same frequencies but with higher power, were also foreseen for use by wide-area networks (WANs). These could link networks around a college or industrial campus without the need for more wiring.

---

160    You can tell a radio geek easily. Ask what 801.11 means. http://www. ieee802.org/11/

By 1998 a host of 802.11b wireless LAN products were being sold, many by major vendors such as Cisco and Intel. They promised 11 Mbps of bandwidth, about the speed of wired Ethernet connections. They promised quick installation for consumers, allowing bedroom computers to share the home-office printer, or modem.

Buyers grabbed these wireless networking products, however, mainly to share their new broadband connections to the Internet around their homes. Wired broadband systems like Digital Subscriber Line (DSL) systems sold by phone companies or cable modems sold by cable companies accessed the Internet at speeds up to 1.5 Mbps, but they were expensive – often $300 to start, and $50 per month. These links were just as expensive as printers, so many buyers bought Wireless LAN kits to share them.

Once they installed their LANs, however, and walked outside to their porches, carrying their laptops, folks discovered something very interesting. Radio waves go through walls, thus wireless links go through walls, too. Wireless LAN access cards worked outdoors. If the DSL link was on, they were on the Internet, at broadband speeds.

It was very cool. The more people investigated it, the cooler it seemed. Just as PCs became a hot hobby in the mid-1970s, so "802.11" networking became a hobbyist fascination in the late 1990s.

## PROGRESS THROUGH PROTOCOLS

At the heart of 802.11 is the idea that equipment is licensed, not users. Once a design shows it meets a standard, anyone can buy it and use it without a further license. This is a contrast to licensed frequencies, where control is placed in the operator or owner of the frequency.

This meant that for WiFi, progress was made by negotiating and implementing new protocols, which equipment makers then supported.

The earliest 802.11b protocols offered a solution for privacy: encryption through what was called Wired Equivalent Privacy (WEP) [161]. This had become an informal standard when the first edition of this

161 WEP is explained at https://en.wikipedia.org/wiki/Wired_Equivalent_Privacy

book was written. A password was used to access a decryption key, and all data going over the air would be encrypted with that key.

By 2004 WEP was superseded by Wi-Fi Protected Access[162], which could be implemented by changing a device's firmware. In 2019 the standard is on its third variation, called WPA3, which uses 128-bit encryption.

As time has passed a host of new IEEE 802.11 standards have emerged:

>> 802.11g, which runs data at 54 Mbps and had become a standard for most WiFi routers by 2010),

>> 802.11n, running data at speeds to 100 Mbps,

>> 802.11u, for interconnecting with cellular sercices

>> 802.11i, a standard for security (802.11i).

Wikipedia maintains a complete list of these standards with links to up-to-date definitions. [163]

## UP IN THE SKY

There's another way to use Moore's Law, apply it to digital radios, and deliver broadband data to consumers.

Instead of putting an antenna on the ground, you can put it in space.

In a 1945 science fiction story the late Arthur C. Clarke (1917-2008)[164] described how a satellite could be placed in a high orbit where it would move at the same speed as the ground underneath it. Its orbit would be synchronized with the rotation of the Earth, and in this "geosynchronous" orbit it would seem to be in one place. Bounce

---

162 WPA is explained at https://en.wikipedia.org/wiki/Wi-Fi_Protected_Access
163     The whole 802.11 rigamarole https://en.wikipedia.org/wiki/IEEE_802.11
164     Yes, you've met him before https://en.wikipedia.org/wiki/Arthur_C._Clarke

signals off this satellite and you can move them around the world very quickly. Moving at the speed of light, such signals can bounce off a satellite 22,300 miles above the Earth in less than a second.

Within 10 years of the Soviet Sputnik launch, communications satellites were going into such geosynchronous orbits. Within 20 years of Sputnik Ted Turner was using satellites to turn his local TV station in Atlanta into a global broadcaster. Satellite TV networks use very, very high frequency bands, around 38 GHz, using directional antennae, at very high power. Once they return, they can be received by low-power antennas, much smaller but still shaped like satellite dishes.

In the 21st century this system has been dramatically impacted by the creative destruction made possible by Moore's Law. Just as magnetic memory gave way to chips, and optical disks gave way to optical fiber networks, so satellites have gone through a re-think.

As this book was being revised, in 2019, the satellite TV companies DirecTv (owned by AT&T) and DISH Network were being made obsolete. Their function in TV was being replaced by optical fiber, WiFi, and faster cellular connections. Their role in moving data, meanwhile, was being made obsolete by constellations of satellites[165] in low-Earth orbit[166] which, like those used in Global Positioning Systems (GPS), aren't stationary but so numerous that small radios can find one.

By 2021 SpaceX CEO Elon Musk had launched hundreds of these satellites and was selling the service under the name Starlink[167]. Amazon and outgoing CEO Jeff Bezos' Blue Origin were launching a similar constellation of satellites called Project Kuiper[168]. The networks are opposed by astronomers who believe they are cutting off their view of the stars.[169]

---

165    An explanation of these satellites is at https://en.wikipedia.org/wiki/Satellite_constellation

166    Low Earth Orbit is low https://en.wikipedia.org/wiki/Low_Earth_orbit

167    Starlink is at https://www.starlink.com/

168    An article on Project Kuiper from the IEEE's tech talk section. https://spectrum.ieee.org/tech-talk/aerospace/satellites/amazons-project-kuiper-is-more-than-the-companys-response-to-spacex

169    An article on the controversy is at https://www.independent.co.uk/life-style/gadgets-and-tech/spacex-launch-latest-starlink-elon-musk-b1071449.html

Low Earth orbit satellite radio is not an entirely new idea. Iridium, a system conceived by Motorola in the late 1980s, sent 66 satellites into orbit with the intention of creating a global telephone service [170]. Their system became operational in 1998. With the expiration of Motorola's patents, and with the improvements in satellite technology made possible by Moore's Law, the way was clear to do things again, only better.

How all this might shake out in 10 years is anyone's guess. The point is that when I first wrote this book WiFi was brand new, that 10 years later it was ubiquitous, and that in 2020 broadband may be ubiquitous around the world, using satellites.

Better and better does indeed get faster and faster.

## SPECTRUM IS AN OCEAN

In a 2001 essay, computer scientist David P. Reed[171] wrote that the electromagnetic spectrum shouldn't be "licensed" and treated as "property" at all.

The whole concept of spectrum regulation is based on a fallacy, he said, the idea that spectrum is like parallel sets of railroad tracks, and that government is required to avoid interference. This led to the idea that spectrum should be licensed, or sold, to private companies.

In fact, the frequency spectrum is more like the ocean, where the use of signals is practically unlimited. The rules should only demand noninterference.

Reed based his argument partly on work done at the University of Illinois, indicating that the capacity of spectrum can be managed so it rises with the number of people using it. This is precisely what has been happening with WiFi. Instead of licensing spectrum, based on its presumed scarcity, he argued, government should simply adopt

---

170    I covered Iridium early in my career. Now it's at https://en.wikipedia.org/wiki/Iridium_satellite_constellation
171    Read about Reed at Wikipedia https://en.wikipedia.org/wiki/David_P._Reed

standards for the use of the spectrum, implemented in hardware and software, assuring the maximum use of the resource, with minimal interference.

The battle between public and private interest, however, still exists, and can ignore science. Comcast, which by the middle of the 2010s was the dominant cable provider, began shipping its customers "free" WiFi routers, which carved out some of the WiFi spectrum for its own use. The result was "Xfinity WiFi, [172]" a service it "gave" its cable customers but sold to everyone else. The public, unlicensed airwaves became partly privatized again.

The technology to make spectrum an ocean, however, is going to come. Thanks to new microprocessors, the products of Moore's Law, and new software, mass-produced inside those chips, and thanks to new methods for using, and delivering, more-and-more data over higher-and-higher frequency bands, the capability of digital radios is growing year-by-year right along with Moore's Law. Moore's Law, in other words, applies to radios.

Bandwidth is unlimited, thanks to Moore's Law of Radios.

---

172    http://wifi.xfinity.com/

# CHAPTER 7

# MOORE'S LAW IS EVERYWHERE

I believe Moore's Law is everywhere. But it doesn't apply everywhere equally, because not all of it is directly dependent on circuit density.

It doesn't apply where there are no computers or means of production that can be transformed using computers, software, and networks. It doesn't apply to the men painting my neighbor's house. They've had to gain productivity in other ways, like replacing brushes with paint sprayers.

But wherever work can be saved with the application of intelligence, you can apply computers and software. There's the chance that the universe may change, a tipping-point reached, so that a revolution begins.

This has happened to many professions over the last 30 years. It happened to my profession of journalism, and to how this book was published, both in its original edition and this updated one. It happened to moviemaking. It happened to lawyers. It happened to photographers. It's happening to bankers, brokers, and all financial intermediaries. It's happening (albeit slowly) to doctors and teachers.

That's because, once something consists of data, and once software for dealing with it is written, the costs of processing it falls dramatically, and the costs of distributing it fall to nothing.

## A JOURNALIST'S STORY

My real introduction to computing came in 1982.

I had used an electric typewriter at my first jobs, as a business reporter for the *Houston Business Journal* and then, the *Birmingham Post-Herald*. (The *Post-Herald* newsroom even had pneumatic tubes to take copy from the copy desk to the composing room.) After being fired by the *Post-Herald* my old bosses took me back, even though Houston's economy had collapsed. My new job was at a paper called the *Atlanta Business Chronicle*.

I had difficulty settling in. I was a young reporter and know-it-all. My old Houston editor, Bill Schadewald, visited and suggested I "start interviewing these high-techies." He meant Atlanta businessmen like Dennis Hayes, founder of Hayes Microcomputer, which made modems until going under in the 1990s, and Leland Strange, then running an add-in board company called Quadram and now CEO of Intelligent Systems, which bought Quadram later that year.

During these interviews, these early PC executives convinced me their products were really going to change the world. They sold me.

The result was that I bought my Kaypro II, a C. Itoh dot-matrix printer, and a 300 baud Anchor Automation modem, for a total of $2,795. I took out a loan to pay for it all.

The Kaypro weighed 26 pounds and was called a luggable. It also had less raw processing power than the calculator my daughter took to high school 20 years later.

The printer made an awful racket and took about one minute to print a page of text using little dots of ink to form letters on fanfold paper. Fanfold pages were perforated on each side of the printed sheet, so you could remove the small holes that moved the paper through the printer.

The modem consumed my phone line whenever it ran, which meant I couldn't talk to someone and use it at the same time. It ran at 300 bits/second, meaning I could read faster than it could deliver words to my Kaypro's screen.

Even by the standards of later in the decade, my Kaypro set-up was comically primitive. But it was still a revolution because nothing like it had existed before in my world.

I hauled this gear between my apartment and the office in my Volkswagen Rabbit, five days a week, for several months. It let me noisily deliver three times the copy of anyone else in the office, all neatly printed for the compositors and lay-out people. They worked at the back of our office, gluing typeset strips onto cardboard frames. The result would be driven to our printer, 50 miles away. I looked forward to the day when my copy would go directly to the editor, and then into print, untouched by human hands. I'm sure the compositors were delighted by my prediction their jobs were about to disappear.

I never saw that day at the *Atlanta Business Chronicle*, because at 28 years old I was loud-mouthed and comically arrogant, with no self-awareness. I thought I knew the business better than my bosses and let them know it. I bragged that I was doing the work of 3 reporters. On March 3 of 1983 the paper laid me off. Three new reporters started the following Monday.

But the revolution couldn't be stopped. A few years after my lay-off the office typewriters did leave, along with the composing machine. A computer network replaced it, where whole newspaper pages could be designed on a screen, then sent to a printer via modem.

By this time, I was writing about technology online, for a service called Newsbytes [173]. I worked on a variety of beats, including a geographic beat covering the U.S. Southeast, one about the phone industry, and on education. I sent my stories via modem and supplemented my pay with freelance assignments for local and national publishers.

In 1994, I got a full-time job for a new magazine called *Interactive Age*. It was created to serve companies manufacturing hardware for two-way cable networks. But my little online page, called the *Interactive Age Daily*, quickly gained a following with Internet news.

The magazine quickly pivoted to Internet coverage and was out of business within a few months, because the cost of paper doubled over the first six months of 1995. In retrospect, how do you cover the business of the Internet in a weekly magazine?

Of course, the revolution was just starting. The Internet was about to take over and, in time, devour the whole journalism business. Few people had a clue.

---

173    I'm glad Wikipedia remembers Newsbytes, because hardly anyone else does.
https://en.wikipedia.org/wiki/Newsbytes_News_Network

At the 1995 Christmas party of the Atlanta Press Club, I still remember how James Cox Kennedy, then CEO of the multi-billion dollar Cox Communications media conglomerate, which owned the *Atlanta Journal-Constitution*, predicted great success by "repurposing" his content for new web sites with names like *Yall.com*, for entertainment.

As he spoke, I hid behind a pillar and laughed until I cried. I considered him "clueless," and was soon writing a weekly newsletter about technology called A-Clue.Com, or A Clue to Internet Commerce.

The fact is that when technology explodes upon an industry it always meets resistance, then adaptation. But resistance is futile, and adaptation only works on technology's terms.

The same forces that turned me from a newspaper and magazine journalist into an online journalist would also hit journalism's side hustle, books.


## A REVOLUTION FOR WRITERS


It took me over six months to draft half my first book, in the early 1990s. (I worked with a coauthor, Lamont Wood, on *Bulletin Board Systems for Business*,[174]. Bulletin boards were a precursor to the Internet revolution, often hosted in people's homes.

Finding references meant conducting interviews, by phone or in person, and traveling to libraries. It was time consuming. It consumed both of us. We had to drop all other work to stay on it. By the end of the process both of us had file drawers filled with papers and notes, arranged by chapter.

The next year I wrote a book about the new field of portable computing, called *A Guide to Field Computing* [175]. I then contributed chapters to books about this new software called a "web browser"

174     Still listed at Amazon, although who would buy it? https://www.amazon.com/Bulletin-Board-Systems-Business-Lamont/dp/0471553484
175     This book was truly ahead of its time, which is why it never made back my advance. https://www.amazon.com/Technology-Edge-Guide-Field-Computing/dp/1562050915

and its HyperText Markup Language (HTML). Each project was all-consuming.

A decade later, thanks to the Internet, the original draft of this book took me just three months to write. And that was part-time – I also did other things. I could keep my Web browser open in a separate window from the text. If I needed to jog my memory or reference something I could use the new Google Toolbar [176].

## THE GOOGLE

By 2001, just three years after its founding, Google maintained a record of discussions on the Usenet, a collection of unaudited discussion threads. These went back to 1985, when I first began working for the *Newsbytes News Service*, which by this time was long forgotten. Google also offered databases of images, news, even a primitive translation service. In 2002, when the first edition of this book went to the printer, Google had revenue of $410 million.[177] By 2010 it had revenue of $28.24 billion and had entered the video market by buying YouTube. (By 2020 YouTube had over 2 billion users according to research at *Business of Apps*. [178] It brought in $28 billion worth of advertising per year by itself.)

I like to say the Web was spun in 1994, because that's when commercial applications for the technology first developed and I started making my living on it, rather than on a dedicated consumer service such as *The Source, CompuServe* or *America Online*, which ran on a phone-based standard called X.25.

A host of search services existed when Google was founded in 1998, from *Yahoo* to *Excite* to *Altavista* and *Ask Jeeves*. Google won by focusing on search, and the needs of search, which dictated the creation

---

176     Even those who remember the Google Toolbar are now middle-aged. https://en.wikipedia.org/wiki/Google_Toolbar

177     This was according to Statista, a research service. https://www.statista.com/statistics/266249/advertising-revenue-of-google/

178     The full Business of Apps report can be found in 2021 at https://www.businessofapps.com/data/youtube-statistics/

of fast computer networks and large computer systems to store data. It was the first search engine whose algorithms, architecture and business model took full advantage of Moore's Law.

Google's architecture split its work up among different servers. Some would conduct queries, some would handle communications, and some just balanced the processing load. It created clusters of these servers around the world and by 2010 had about 450,000 of them. But they are all just Intel x86 PCs, the same as you could buy in a store, loaded into racks, and connected using the Ethernet cable you could buy for a home network.

But as it was doing this Google also helped create "The Cloud."

Google has more than doubled my writing productivity. But it hasn't doubled everyone's. Most writers aren't as dependent on finding Web pages as I am. When I wrote fiction, Google didn't speed my work at all. The main service provided me by Moore's Law for most of my life is that of a typewriter. Mark Twain used a typewriter almost 150 years ago. And no typewriter will turn you, nor I, into Mark Twain.

## WIKIPEDIA

Most references in this book are to pages on a Web site that launched as I was beginning to write the first edition of this book.

The web site is called Wikipedia, whose main page is at https://en.wikipedia.org.

Wikipedia launched in January 2001 as a "user-written encyclopedia." Its Wiki system was designed to let anyone write, or rewrite, information on any subject and stores the results for retrieval. There are many Wikis today, and you can easily create one to organize a project for work or school.

Wikipedia is only as honest as the people writing for it, and as accurate as the people editing it. Because it depends on the wisdom of crowds, it has been subject to many controversies.

Here are two that occurred between the first and second editions of the book:

- **The Seigenthaler Incident**[179] -- Someone posted a hoax about American journalist John Seigenthaler, accusing him (among other things) of involvement in the Kennedy Assassination. It took four months to correct it. Wikipedia responded by stopping anonymous users from creating new articles.
- **The Essjay Controversy**[180] – A Wikipedia editor named Ryan Jordan, who used Essjay as a username, was found to have falsified his resume, and used the credential to influence Wikipedia policy. He was also a source for a negative profile of the service in the *New Yorker*. Jordan resigned.

To its credit the pages of Wikipedia are honest about these controversies and detail the criticisms honestly. But there has been negative reaction to Wikipedia's mistakes and its open editing policies. Some groups objecting to Wikipedia, and the way it is run, have since used the Wiki software to create their own online encyclopedia, using different rules for participants.[181]

Despite the efforts of critics, Wikipedia had by 2019 replaced most encyclopedias. The transformation was helped by a 2005 study that found Wikipedia to be as accurate as the latest *Encyclopedia Britannica*, even when incidents like that involving Seigenthaler were accounted for.

There is another advantage of Wikipedia, one which made it possible for the 2010 edition to be a true Internet Book.

The page on Mark Twain will remain fixed where it is, at https://en.wikipedia.org/wiki/Mark_Twain. It may change but it won't move. I use Wikipedia links wherever possible. Corporations go out of business, or just change their priorities. Publishers change policies. Pages are

179     Wikipedia retains a page on this incident https://en.wikipedia.org/wiki/Wikipedia_Seigenthaler_biography_incident
180     I am glad Wikipedia maintains pages about its controversies, because otherwise they might be forgotten and regularly repeated. https://en.wikipedia.org/wiki/Essjay_controversy
181     Wikipedia's own list of Wikis https://en.wikipedia.org/wiki/List_of_wikis

moved regularly. This makes link references difficult to incorporate in a book. It's a concept called Link Rot. [182]

But Wikipedia links abide. I changed many links from the First Edition to Wikipedia pages, for just this reason. It had nothing to do with Wikipedia's accuracy, everything to do with its stability.

## Publishers Miss the Revolution

What happens to industries that resist the implications of Moore's Law, that can't or won't adjust?

Publishing is just such an industry.

What happens is these industries become niche, bespoke, quaint, then antique. They can disappear.

In 1991 a book could turn a profit easily on a "press run" of 20,000 copies, especially in the computer press, where I worked. At $20 per book, a run of 20,000 brought in $400,000. The retailers took half, the distributors took a hefty cut, but there was still enough to pay for writers, editors, marketing, and printing.

By 2001 that was no longer true. The rising cost of manufacturing books – the paper, the ink, the printing, the transportation – squeezed budgets. The costs of marketing books also rose as the attention paid to books by the media declined. The book selling "channel" by then was dominated by the Barnes & Noble chain, by Amazon.Com and other online retailers, and by new outlets like airport bookshops.

The result was that fewer books made a profit.

The "best-sellers" could still sell themselves, either through the author's name or the presumed author's name (as when a public figure has a book ghost-written for them). Editors had to become marketers, writers were left on their own and there was no room for the "midlist"

---

182     Link rot is why most publishers remain reluctant to put Internet references in non-fiction books. I published this book myself. https://en.wikipedia.org/wiki/Link_rot

author, the journeyman (or woman) whose work might sell 20,000 copies at a time, with proper support.

# E-Books

For these authors one answer was the "E-book."

E-books cost almost nothing to reproduce. They can be distributed electronically.

The e-book industry grew quickly between 2001-2010. By 2019 there was only one name to know, the Amazon.Com Kindle. Even Microsoft turned off its e-book system in 2019, destroying at a keystroke thousands of books people once thought they had bought.[183] (To its credit, Microsoft gave refunds to victims of its decision.[184])

There were still complaints about Amazon's Kindle readers in 2010, four years after their introduction. By 2019, while Kindle e-book readers were still being sold, Amazon was also offering Kindle books on its Fire Tablets, costing as little as $50 each, and as a free app for phones.

The last product competing with the Kindle is the Barnes & Noble Nook. It is made by the same Chinese company that makes the iPhone.[185] The book chain behind it was sold to a hedge fund operator for just $638 million.[186] (The Nook was still being sold in 2021.[187])

---

183    NPR covered this story like it was a horror movie. https://www.npr.org/2019/07/07/739316746/microsoft-closes-the-book-on-its-e-library-erasing-all-user-content

184    The Microsoft refunds got a lot less publicity. https://www.thurrott.com/cloud/web-browsers/microsoft-edge/209098/microsoft-ebook-refunds-coming-in-july

185    A 2019 story about the Nook https://goodereader.com/blog/barnes-and-noble-nook-ereader-news/banes-and-noble-nook-sales-fell-17-1-in-2019

186    *Forbes* covered the sale https://www.forbes.com/sites/lawrencelight/2019/06/24/the-barnes-noble-buyout-a-godsend-for-book-readers-and-investors/#52bc94bef8f8

187    https://www.barnesandnoble.com/b/nook/_/N-1pbl

# Self-Publishing

The first edition of this book was self-published through a company called Trafford Publishing. I delivered the computer file over the Internet, and Trafford printed a bunch of copies. They also kept the file online to print additional orders, from me, from stores, or from individuals.

It was left to me to market the book. I'm a writer, not a marketer. While I have written about marketing, I would much rather be writing a story.

Traditional book publishers sold books through catalogs, through displays sent to bookstores that stocked the book, and personal appearances by the author. Media campaigns, whether print, radio, or television, turned authors into celebrities, and the agents who could arrange such appearances more than earned their fees.

The demise of newspapers, the decline of magazines, and the rising culture of celebrity caused a merger between mass-market publishing and the celebrity industry by 2010. Every celebrity worth talking to had to have a book. This created work for "ghost" writers, but these writers got no credit for the work.

In 2019 Amazon dominated both the market for self-published books as well as e-books. Formatted books could be produced through the same system, called KDP Select, [188] which was used for e-books.

While nostalgia brought back some local bookstores, and libraries still existed, it was clear by 2019 the industry was now Amazon's to control. On the other hand, this book was as easy to publish as sending the file to Amazon and choosing a cover and price.

In 2021 things are even easier for the e-book writer. The primary purpose of owning a physical book is nostalgic. The primary reason to visit a bookstore is serendipity, the hope of stumbling upon something great and unexpected.

---

[188]    KDP Select is at http://kdp.amazon.com

## Moore's Law in Perverse: Education

Perhaps no industry has seen more of the perverse impacts of Moore's Law than education. Few have fought it so successfully.

I covered education technology starting in the late 1980s, when my first child was born. Educators were being offered great-new computers and great-new software. Each generation was better than the one before. Sometimes the new machines cost less than those they replaced.

But it was a trap. While PCs were great, they quickly became obsolete. Within a very few years "forward-thinking" educators who had pushed teachers and administrators into buying PCs found themselves looking at tons of useless iron, running obsolete software. Students had better computers, and software, at home.

For many years, in education, Moore's Law ran in perverse. Money spent on technology was wasted money. This greatly increased the "digital divide" – the technology distance between the wealthy and the poor. Poor kids either had old technology or none.

When the Internet appeared on elementary school desktops, in the mid-1990s, many schools were thus reluctant to adopt it. Some actively resisted the Internet, for many years, calling it dangerous. Some insisted the Internet run on PCs they already had – even if those PCs couldn't run common browsers.

The industry didn't help. PC companies like Dell urged schools to buy expensive laptops for their schools. Their TV ads showed a cart, filled with laptops, teachers handing out those laptops, and schoolrooms turned into "computer labs."

For educators it was a dream but for administrators, a nightmare. The computers in that Dell commercial would cost the school $20,000 per classroom, and they, too, would become obsolete quickly.

What elementary education really needed was the Internet, but a mature Internet.

The Internet would let teachers share insights and deliver grades quickly to a central office. It would let teachers stay in touch with students (and parents), especially if there are computers at home. With Internet connectivity, schools and students no longer had to get the latest-and-greatest hardware.

I saw this play out when my kids were in high school. Only after my daughter graduated in 2006 did a workable solution appear – Linux based terminals with cheap flat screens, connected to a central server and then to the Internet. The value came from the wire they were connected to. Within a few years the wires became obsolete as WiFi improved.

Once networking became widespread, another Moore's Law perversion came about. Colleges and universities became convinced networks could replace their campuses. Many put their curricula online. New kinds of for-profit universities emerged, like the so-called University of Phoenix, that were entirely Web-based. By 2009 UP was big enough to have naming rights on the Arizona Cardinals' football stadium.

But these schools weren't for everyone. Anyone can use the Web to learn, but those who aren't self-directed learners need real teachers. Many schools have since pulled-back from Web education experiments.

Moore's Law, by itself, isn't revolutionizing education. The cost of education keeps rising. It's still a people-intensive business. But even in 2019, this story is not over.

Other industries are using Moore's Law, not to improve their productivity, but to slow it down. An example is the legal profession.

## MOORE'S LAW IN PERVERSE: THE LAW

Productivity can have a perverse effect. In the law productivity means you can create a lot more motions, and a lot more evidence. It doesn't mean trials cost less, and it doesn't necessarily make justice better.

The first working PC I ever saw was a Cromemco Z-80, which a neighbor bought while I was still pounding-out stories with an IBM Selectric typewriter at the *Houston Business Journal*, in 1979.[189] My neighbor transcribed court records with the computer, and hired friends to do the same, sending their results to her via modem for printing.

This was just the start of a revolution.

A few years later I was in Atlanta, and one of my "tech" stories was about a start-up called Information America. (The company is now part of Thomson-Reuters' Westlaw.[190]) A local entrepreneur was making deals with local courthouses, putting their court records online and paying them a portion of the access fees those records generated. Instead of sending couriers to the courthouse, paying for copies to be made, then having them delivered back to an office, lawyers could access those records from their desks, or more often their librarians could. Online access cost less than couriers, and the entrepreneur made money.

Lots of other records were going online at the same time, through Westlaw and Reed-Elsevier's Lexis-Nexis,[191] which also held a database of news articles. Legal offices were putting their records into local area networks and turning those files into databases. Soon lawyers began accessing these records from own desks, then from laptops.

By the time of the O.J. Simpson trial [192] in 1996, courtrooms looked very different than they did in 1983, when I became a freelancer. Judge Lance Ito kept a laptop on his desk. The whole jury room was networked. That trial was also the first chance many people had to see how computer-driven forensics was transforming criminal law. DNA evidence was a critical component for the prosecution, and skepticism about its handling was a vital part of the defense case.

Despite all this technology, all this access to information, the trial took nine months. Productivity hasn't cut the cost of the law. The tools

---

189    The Cromemco company is forgotten now. It shouldn't be. Here is Wikipedia's page on Cromemco. https://en.wikipedia.org/wiki/Cromemco

190    Westlaw is at https://legal.thomsonreuters.com/en/products/westlaw

191    Lexis-Nexis is at https://www.lexisnexis.com/en-us/home.page

192    This is one Wikipedia page I wish didn't exist. https://en.wikipedia.org/wiki/O._J._Simpson_murder_case

created an "arms race" in which legal costs ratchet up-and-up. A 2001 survey by the American Intellectual Property Lawyers' Association (AIPLA) found that some courts were taking 22 months to try patent cases, and trials with under $25 million at risk were costing each litigant about $1.5 million

There aren't just problems when justice is delayed. Technology can also deny justice. It takes a lot of money to take a rich litigant to trial, whether in civil or criminal court. This causes district attorneys to refrain from trying rich people. It can prevent justice from being done in civil court.

While industries like the law struggle with the impact of Moore's Law, others are transformed without seeming to change at all.

Take the movies, for instance.

## MOORE ON THE BIG SCREEN

Computers and networks can improve the productivity of creative people. But productivity isn't measured only in output per hour.

Sometimes computing can completely change the nature of the creative process, and the creative output. This is what happened in animation and special effects as the first edition of this book was being written.

Before the 1990s, animated movies were often called "cartoons." They were created with an analog process. A director would draw cartoon panels with the plot of the final product, producing a "story board." By the 1960s these would be sent to the Far East, where vast teams of artists would draw the backgrounds, the characters, and the cells depicting each scene. Then would come the assembly, with the music and voices added in a studio.

The process by which such movies as *Beauty and the Beast* were produced wasn't much different from that used by Walt Disney himself to produce *Steamboat Willie*. The main difference was the use of Asian artists.

The first "Star Wars" pictures were hints of what was to come. Director George Lucas wanted to push the state-of-the-art in computer animation. The first movie in the series looked primitive next to the third because of his extensive use of computers. Lucas created his own special effects group within his LucasFilm production company called Industrial Light & Magic.[193] The computer graphics unit of that company was later sold to Apple Computer co-founder Steve Jobs in 1986 and renamed Pixar.[194]

Under Jobs, Pixar produced animation software called Renderman to speed the process of delivering computer animation, not only for itself but for others. (Renderman was given a special Oscar in 2001. [195])

Pixar followed up the launch of Renderman by signing a contract to produce feature-length films for Disney in 1991. This culminated in 1995 with the release of the movie *Toy Story*, which broke box office records. (The previous year's biggest animated hit, *The Lion King*, was produced using the older process.)

Pixar movies soon began bringing in more money than traditional animation. Disney closed its hand-drawn animation unit, starting in 2004, and bought Pixar in 2006. Steve Jobs' widow, Laurene Powell Jobs, remained Disney's largest shareholder until 2017.

Since 2010 computer animation has come to dominate what was formerly considered the "live action" movie genre. By 2019 all the 25 top-grossing pictures of all time were heavy users of computer animation.[196] The list was led by 2009's *Avatar*.

Many movies intended for theaters in 2019 were based on comic books, making extensive use of computer graphics. Most acting was being conducted in front of green screens, and the actors have no idea

193    ILM was one of the most important business stories in Hollywood history https://en.wikipedia.org/wiki/Industrial_Light_%26_Magic
194    The Wikipedia page on Pixar https://en.wikipedia.org/wiki/Pixar
195    The Wikipedia page on Renderman https://en.wikipedia.org/wiki/Pixar_RenderMan
196    The complete list is at http://mentalfloss.com/article/581606/highest-grossing-movies-all-time-worldwide

what the final product would look like. These movies are derisively called "Spandex" movies in the trade, because of the form-fitting costumes. But they bring in the money.

Spandex movies cost more to produce than movies using just actors and sets. Computer graphics created an "arms race" in the movie business, which continues to drive engineering creativity. Scripts, direction, acting, all the ingredients that once made for Hollywood success, no longer matter in 2019. Not if you want to put people into chairs at $10-15 each, $30 if you include popcorn and a drink.

In 2021 excitement was building about an even-newer technology, Epic Studios' Unreal Engine. Originally created to deliver 3D effects to video games, movie studios were starting to use it for filming on special "smart stages," surrounding the actors with the equivalent of a green screen and having them interact directly with images that could "enter" the scene. [197]

The result will be movies with far more depth, and the opportunity to deliver them in new types of immersive "theaters" that may look nothing like the movie theater you went to a few years ago.

## Moore in Your Camera

When the first edition of this book was published the analog-digital conversion was hitting photography full-force. The first digital camera I bought, in 1999, could only capture 100,000 pixels in a single photo. While I was able to make pictures for my personal website with this camera, portrait-quality photos were still taken with a "chemical-based" analog camera, then transferred to a digital standard like .jpeg.

But Moore's Law has taken over. Improvements in digital photography have come faster-and-faster. By 2008, when my wife and I sat for a formal portrait, we faced a small digital camera on a tripod. After dozens of pictures were taken with this camera, we were ushered into a second room, where a salesman showed us the images on a screen

197    The main web page for the Unreal Engine is at https://www.unrealengine.com/en-US/

and took our order. He was able to show us precisely how various types of digital effects would look applied to the finished product.

Olan-Mills, the company which took those pictures, didn't last much longer. It was bought by a company called LifeTouch in 2011, which closed the company's facilities in Chattanooga in 2012. [198]

Kodak, the leader in chemical photography for generations, dropped its line of Kodachrome film in 2009 and survived in 2019, barely, because it went into digital photography. Polaroid, which pioneered "instant" photography in the 1960s, went bankrupt in 2001. Today grandparents can get copies of all their grandkids' digital photos and update them via WiFi.

In 2019, the still camera business was dying entirely, photography becoming a feature inside devices like the iPhone 11. All the photography and film stores near my home in Atlanta had closed. One is now a yoga studio.

## MOORE IN DISTRIBUTION

Moore's Law hit the worlds of retailing and distribution along with PCs and change there has been accelerating.

I detailed some of it in *A Guide to Field Computing.*" (The book is now, sadly, out of print. Since it came out before the Web was spun in 1994, the digital files have also disappeared.) The most amazing fact in that book was that the amount of warehouse space in the U.S. hadn't risen since the late 1970s. Much of this was covered in Chapter 3.

The chief 20th century beneficiary of barcode technology was Walmart. While the company's histories emphasize folksy founder Sam Walton, his religious values, or the corporate emphasis on low prices, Walmart was a technology story.

Sam Walton originally offered low prices by buying in bulk and offering customers minimal help in picking through the piles

---

198     Fortunately I still have the pictures https://en.wikipedia.org/wiki/Olan_Mills

of merchandise. But his company's success was based on its data warehouse, not its physical warehouses.

Walmart had a huge database of merchandise, a huge network of suppliers, and a physical network of stores, warehouses, and trucks. But databases told it precisely what was on its shelves in every store, allowing it to adjust merchandising to local conditions. The company's physical network then moved products from factories to the stores.

This let Walmart find a new way to profit. Back then, most retailers bought on a "60-day net" basis. They had to pay for stock within two months of getting it. This matched the speed with which retailers would sell-out, or "turn over," that inventory. After that, the merchant would put it on sale to pay the bill. Since the retail price was usually twice what the product cost to buy from the manufacturer, the retailer would still draw a profit.

Walmart's data warehousing system let it turn over its inventory in just two weeks. In other words, it began selling what it bought six weeks before having to pay for it. Walmart could invest its inventory cost for six weeks before sending out the check.

Walmart's success launched an era of "big box" retailing. Home Depot and Lowe's used Walmart techniques to sell hardware and related products. Toys R Us did it in toys, Best Buy n electronics, Petsmart in pet products, Staples in office supplies.

Then came Amazon.

## Mass Customization

Since 2002 retailing has been overthrown by mass customization and e-commerce.

Michael Dell was demonstrating this back in the late 20th century. Instead of selling computers in stores, he sold them online or by phone. Customers could get the precise set-up they needed, and Dell's U.S. factory could then produce each machine to order. As I wrote at the time, PCs are like rotting fruit, their value declining as they sat on a loading dock. By selling PCs to order, Dell got full value from his parts and turned over his inventory quickly. Sometimes, as with Walmart, he could sell parts before he bought them.

Amazon.Com took this one step further. Its warehouses stock millions of items. It makes maximum use of robots to pick orders, pack them, and ship them from those warehouses. Huge investments in technology and delivery infrastructure let Amazon "break bulk" on merchandise without putting it on a shelf, where it might be stolen.

One by one, Amazon replaced many of the big boxes. Toys R Us went bankrupt in 2017. Staples went private the same year. In 2019, other big boxes were threatened by online-only merchants like Casper in mattresses, Chewy in pet supplies, and Stitch Fix in clothing. Those stores that survived, like Best Buy, have done so by selling services, not just products.

Many more store chains died during the COVID-19 pandemic. Some were kept alive, in zombie fashion, as mall owner Simon Property Group partnered with Authentic Brands, a branding company, to keep them open. When I went to get my own COVID vaccine shot, in early 2021, it was at Simon mall that was slowly being turned into a medical clinic.

In his last letter to shareholders before stepping down as CEO, early in 2021 [199] Jeff Bezos estimated his Prime customers saved $126 billion in 2020 alone by not having to go to stores for merchandise. I'm an Amazon Prime member and I don't dispute it.


## Moore Puts Your Doc in a box

In the first edition of this book, I wrote "Moore's Law has changed the way we practice medicine but has not yet changed the way we consume it."

---

199      The Bezos letter is here https://www.aboutamazon.com/news/company-news/2020-letter-to-shareholders

In the 20 years since this has begun to change.

The most important changes made possible by Moore's Law are Electronic Health Records (EHRs) and Personal Health Records (PHRs). Both are made possible by the lower networking costs and Internet access costs that became common, thanks to Moore's Law, in the years since 2001.

Many people get PHRs and EHRs confused, and the difference is mainly a legal one:

- An **EHR** is created by your doctor or your hospital. It belongs to them. It describes their visits with you, their diagnosis, and your treatment. EHRs are subject to a federal law called HIPAA (The Health Information Portability and Accountability Act[200], passed in 1996. In practice, this means you sign a lot more forms when you see a new doctor, or go to a different hospital, even see a new pharmacist.

- A **PHR** is supposed to belong to you. In theory it would pack as many EHRs as you created with your various doctors. It could also include data you create yourself, from a fitness tracker like FitBit logging your sleep to an app on your Apple Watch checking your sugar levels. Both Google and Microsoft tried to compete in the PHR space, but quickly abandoned the field.

In early 2009, the Obama Administration tried to jumpstart the EHR and PHR movement through a law called HITECH (Health Information Technology for Economic and Clinical Health [201]), part of its economic stimulus package. HITECH provided $19 billion of what I came to call "sweet, sweet stimulus cash" for doctors to automate health records by 2014, along with penalties (in the form of lower Medicare payments) for those that didn't. The act set off a gold rush by vendors eager to sell their wares.

200    Learn more about HIPAA at https://en.wikipedia.org/wiki/Health_Insurance_Portability_and_Accountability_Act
201    Learn more about the HiTech Act at https://en.wikipedia.org/wiki/Health_Information_Technology_for_Economic_and_Clinical_Health_Act.

Unfortunately, many EHR projects conducted under HITECH were failures. Many hospitals and clinics did not choose cloud-based systems. Instead, they installed expensive computers inside their offices. These systems were often incompatible with one another. The complexity of the law, and HIPAA rules, drove all but specialty companies from the market. I'm still filling out paper forms each time I see a new doctor, in 2021.

As was true in education, professional resistance by health providers has put Moore's Law in perverse.

We will talk more about that when we address Moore's Law of Software in Chapter Nine.

# Chapter 8

# Moore's Law vs. AT&T

Moore's Law creates technology debt. The value of old systems and old systems constantly goes down.

To stay competitive, companies must pay this "technology debt" or fail.

AT&T is a case study of it.

Technology debt is the cost of using old tools and the cost of upgrading to new tools. I discussed this in Chapter Seven, in terms of various industries and professions.

In the 21$^{st}$ century you must use computers to get business done, but computers change. Networking changes. User interfaces change. Thus, computing requires continual investment in hardware, software, and services. Anyone failing to keep up increases their technology debt.

This process can destroy enormous companies, and thousands of jobs at a time. Government can't protect against this.

Government antitrust policies, in fact, accelerate the destruction. Coming down on a company because it is abusing temporary market power puts it into a defensive crouch, leaving it vulnerable to the accelerating change that is the hallmark of Moore's Law.

This is what happened to Microsoft. It fought the U.S. government in court, finally signed a consent decree covering its future actions, and spent almost 15 years in the background of the technology business. It didn't begin to grow again until after the decree was lifted.

I witnessed this first-hand.

When WiFi became a force in 2004, I was hired to help produce a white paper for Microsoft, about the opportunity to make WiFi routers, which would be sold through telephone and cable companies. I even traveled to Microsoft's Redmond, WA headquarters to present the idea.

The idea went nowhere. Microsoft executives feared the antitrust implications of the idea. They didn't feel the risk was worthwhile.

Fortunately, the consent decree was lifted in 2011. Microsoft committed its future to the cloud three years later. In 2021 it was the third most-valuable company on the planet, behind only Apple and Saudi Arabia's national oil company.

When it comes to technology debt, a refusal to participate in the future is not an option. Only a few paths lead to success. Most companies fail, including the largest companies.

Nowhere is this plainer than in the case of AT&T, whose fortunes I have followed professionally for over 40 years. The company built around Alexander Graham Bell's invention in the 19th century, became the regulated Bell System in the 20th century, was broken up in 1984 because it was too powerful, and was destroyed a second time in the 21st century by Moore's Law.

Can Moore's Law of Radios save it?

I don't know. But let's start this story at the beginning.


## THE COPPER MIRACLE

AT&T was built on the miracle of copper.

Copper is not a semiconductor. Copper conducts electricity. It's also inexpensive, especially compared to gold, which is a better conductor.

Copper was a great triumph of the 19th century. Most of the world I grew up with, before Moore's Law took hold of our lives, was based on copper.

Copper's properties were first seen in the experiments of Michael Faraday, 1791-1867. [202] Faraday created "electromagnetic induction"

---

202    Learn about Michael Faraday at Wikipedia https://en.wikipedia.org/wiki/Michael_Faraday

– inducing an electric current in one wire from the electromagnetic field created by a current running over an adjacent wire. The ability to control electricity through magnetism was one of the 19th century's great discoveries.

The painter Samuel Morse, 1791-1872[203] turned Faraday's lesson, and his own publicity skills, into a contract from the U.S. government to produce the first working intercity telegraph, tapping out "What hath God wrought?" using a dot-and-dash code, later named Morse Code for him, from Washington to Baltimore.

As great as the impact of the Internet is, it pales in comparison to Moore's telegraph. (This is detailed in a great book by Tom Standage, *The Victorian Internet*.[204] I mention it twice because it's that good.) The telegraph entered a world where communication meant semaphores, fast horses, and pigeons. Telegraphy brought us the first technology "nerds." Trained operators were needed to work the telegraph, listening for the codes, transcribing them onto paper, and tapping them out to pass messages along. The best operators were valued much as star computer programmers are today.

The best-known of these early operators was Thomas Edison (1847-1931)[205]. He had been left nearly deaf by scarlet fever and this made it possible for him to work the line without distraction, leaning his good ear into the mechanism.

Edison saw that the miracle wasn't the telegraph, but electricity running through a wire. Edison was a scientific rock star, his career founded on harnessing the power of electricity in such things as the light bulb, the phonograph, and the movie camera. Edison's lab at Menlo Park was an inspiration, like the garages of 20th century tech entrepreneurs in Silicon Valley. He made the mold, and in the process inspired other

203     Samuel Morse the painter is now forgotten. Samuel Morse the "inventor" is at Wikipedia https://en.wikipedia.org/wiki/Samuel_Morse
204     The Standage book on telegraphy is not only great history but a great read. https://www.amazon.com/Victorian-Internet-Remarkable-Nineteenth-line/dp/162040592X
205     Edison was played as a young man by Mickey Rooney, as an older man by Spencer Tracy, and as an entry in Wikipedia https://en.wikipedia.org/wiki/Thomas_Edison

tinkerers, like Bell, to build their own workshops.

As a businessman, Edison made many mistakes. He depended heavily on the monopolies that his patents gave him. They made him disdainful of those who could improve on his inventions or exploit them in a competitive market. The movie industry moved to California in part because Edison's attorneys chased it there.

Another mistake was Edison's belief in Direct Current for power. His Edison Electric was a predecessor to today's General Electric. But the world wasn't ready at that time for homes and businesses to have their own power generators, something solar panels make possible today.

Nikola Tesla, who was mentioned in Chapter Six, *Moore's Law of Radios*, had a better idea for moving with Alternating Current, or A/C. A/C let power be created in central generators and transmitted efficiently hundreds of miles to where it was needed. (The fight over DC and AC current is the plot of the 2019 movie *The Current Wars*.)

The biggest business mistake of the 19th century, however, wasn't made by Edison but by the Western Union Co., which then dominated telegraphy. Alexander Graham Bell and his partners offered the telephone patents to Western Union for $100,000.[206]

Western Union rejected the offer. Monopoly, whether it's regulated or unregulated, makes the monopolist lazy.

## The First AT&T

Bell's telephone and Tesla's A/C power created enormous demand for copper. They transformed the world as nothing else had before (and as nothing has since). Late 19th century New York City became crisscrossed with copper wire.

The world of copper created huge new industries requiring vast amounts of capital. This transformed capitalism itself. The needs of

---

206     The Guardian newspaper wrote about this in 2007 https://www. theguardian.com/technology/2007/aug/06/bellvwestern

industry, and the inefficiency of having competing wires from several suppliers competing over the same ground, demanded the creation of regulated monopolies.

The same process was happening throughout industry in the early 20th century. Controlled monopolies could use scarce capital efficiently, allowing new industries to be created with money that would otherwise be spent competing. This was the "Age of Trusts," business combinations put together by Wall Street bankers in steel, oil, electricity, local transport, natural gas, and telecommunications.

In exchange for negotiated rates, monopolists promised to offer service to everyone, and at the lowest possible cost.

The father of the telecommunications monopoly called Bell System is nearly forgotten today, but he is very important to business history. His name was Theodore Newton Vail [207].

Vail had worked with Bell's father-in-law, Gardiner Hubbard, to build the American Bell Telephone Co., the predecessor of AT&T, which defended Bell's patents. He pioneered the use of copper in phone wires. He retired in 1889 but returned in 1907 to lead the fight to create a Bell System monopoly, writing personal, revealing letters in the company's annual report that were precursors to those of Warren Buffett in the 20th century and Jeff Bezos in the 21st.

Along the way Vail also created the concept of public relations. His spokesmen told the public, through both free and paid media, that AT&T was not just trying to maximize profit but improve society. The Bell System promise was that in exchange for monopoly status and limits on profits, AT&T and its partners would offer "universal service," giving the most rural communities the same access to the world market as someone in New York.

This is the communications system I grew up with. The Bell System owned the phone in my house (in the LIncoln 1 exchange) and at Tower TV (PYramid 8). It still owned the phone I used when I bought my current house in 1983. (I still use the number.)

---

207    Vail is almost completely forgotten today. He shouldn't be. https://en.wikipedia.org/wiki/Theodore_Newton_Vail

Bell System phones were safe, efficient, and you could reach anyone with them. They let me continue my work as a reporter even after losing my newspaper job in 1983. When I made a long-distance call, I would log it in a notebook. When the bill came, I would match each call to the publication I made it for, sending each publisher a detailed bill.

There was one big thing wrong with the Bell System. It was an analog service. Once digital services became commonplace, it was doomed.

## THE LAST COPPER MONOPOLY

Cable television in the U.S. was also, originally, an analog service.

It dates from the late 1940s, when television was getting its start.[208]

When I attended the late Dick Clark's [209] induction into broadcasting's Hall of Fame, in the 1990s, he went on at-length during his speech about his early efforts to become a cable operator. His idea was to use big antennas to transmit New York's stations to his own Philadelphia area and sell them there. The correct model turned out to be re-transmitting programs from Philadelphia stations to points like Williamsport, where the broadcast was blocked by surrounding hills.

Throughout the 1950s and 1960s cable was a slow-growth industry, based on these original concepts. It was called community access television (CATV) because it brought city programs to small towns that couldn't reach them using the small roof antennas I installed for my dad at Tower TV.

The 1970s saw the development of most of what we now consider basic cable technology. For consumers, the heart of it was a "set-top" box on top of the TV, and a remote control that let consumers switch among the various channels with a remote control. (My first remote in 1980 used a wire, later ones used an infrared sensor and beam.)

---

208    The Wikipedia history of cable TV https://en.wikipedia.org/wiki/Cable_television_in_the_United_States

209    Hard to believe Clark is nearly forgotten, just 20 years later. But refresh your memory https://en.wikipedia.org/wiki/Dick_Clark

The most important thing Cable TV delivered was coaxial cable[210], an invention credited in 1929 to Lloyd Espenshied and Herman Affel of AT&T. Coax could carry more signals across more frequencies than the single-clad copper or steel AT&T itself was using. Rather than replacing those wires, however, AT&T kept them. I still had one running past my Atlanta home as late as the mid-1990s. Coaxial cable, on the other hand, consists of a thick copper wire surrounded by insulation, then a copper mesh acting as a ground, then more insulation. It connects to a set (or another cable) through a connector that screws-in from the outside until tight.

Telephone companies had long used "coax" for long-distance lines since it could transmit many calls simultaneously over great distances with minimal loss. Cable entrepreneurs applied "coax" to local service, using its bandwidth to broadcast as many channels as they could.

Just as a painter, Samuel F.B. Morse, was instrumental in the development of telegraphy it was a writer, Arthur C. Clarke, was instrumental in the development of later cable television service. Some of what follows was covered, briefly, in Chapter 6.

Clarke wrote a short piece for a magazine called *Wireless World*[211] in 1945, proposing the concept of "geosynchronous satellites." He wrote that if a satellite were placed in an orbit that matched the speed of the turning Earth, it would stay over the same location and communication signals could be bounced off it reliably.

While the "Space Race" of the 1960s is remembered today for putting Neil Armstrong on the Moon, it was also about making Clarke's idea a reality. The first Soviet satellite, Sputnik, was a communications beacon. Walter Cronkite broadcast the first "live by satellite" pictures from the Telstar satellite in 1962. NASA's geosynchronous satellite program was called Syncom.[212] Syncom 2, launched in July 1963, was its first success, and debuted with a telephone call between President John F. Kennedy and Nigeria's Prime Minister. Armstrong's steps were transmitted live, around the world, using a network of geosynchronous

210     Coaxial cable, or coax, is one of the great inventions of its time. https://en.wikipedia.org/wiki/Coaxial_cable

211     Someone saved the article. http://lakdiva.org/clarke/1945ww/

212     Wikipedia on Syncom https://en.wikipedia.org/wiki/Syncom

satellites.

By the 1970s geosynchronous satellites, based on Clarke's principle, were repeating voice and data as well as TV signals. Home Box Office was the first channel to deliver its signal to affiliated cable networks via satellite. It was quickly followed by Ted Turner's WTBS and Pat Robertson's CBN.

By 1980 cable had become what I call "the last copper gold rush." Giant corporations teamed with local political leaders to carve out city franchises. I was able to see Houston's map as it was being negotiated. My editor at that time said later he was amazed not to see anything scandalous in it. These franchises would take billions of dollars to "build out" but it was assumed they would offer an endless stream of monopoly profits.

What few people realized was that the technology they were using contained its own "Achilles Heel," a fatal flaw that would, in time, create overwhelming competition in cable's own niche of re-transmitting TV signals.

The Achilles Heel was copper.

## The Full Service Network

In 1994 I was finishing my nine-year run at Newsbytes, a technology news service which was later part of the Washington Post Co. A lot of the talk on my telecommunications beat involved a Time Warner Cable experiment in Orlando called the "Full-Service Network," [213] aimed at testing the limits of interactive TV. It was the successor to a 1976 experiment called QUBE[214] in Columbus, Ohio which had resulted in the creation of many channels we take for granted today, including the Nickelodeon channel for children.

---

213    The FSN was a big deal for a very short time https://en.wikipedia.org/wiki/
Full_Service_Network#Time_Warner_TV_Venture_in_Florida_1994_to_1997
214    QUBE was a very big deal when I was in college. https://en.wikipedia.org/
wiki/QUBE

The idea behind the FSN experiment was to spend millions of dollars upgrading the cable plant of 4,000 subscribers and see just how much money the operator could extract from consumers as a result. The system featured games, online shopping, and a video-on-demand service. I described a little of what happened next in Chapter 7.

CMP Media Inc. decided to get in on the ground floor and create a new magazine to cover the technology, which it called "*Interactive Age.*" David Klein, editor of the broadcasting trade magazine "*Electronic Media,*" was hired to head the effort. I had worked for David at his previous job, writing a column on computer technology for TV station managers, and we were friends. He hired me to launch the magazine's online effort, a news page (based on my previous Newsbytes work) that would debut along with the print edition on October 26, 1994.

As I searched for news on interactive cable, however, I found something far more interesting to cover in the Internet. The first Web browsers were coming into use. The limits on commercial use of the Internet were about to be lifted. All sorts of companies were experimenting with new "Web sites," and consumers were dialing-up to the new medium over phone lines, using hundreds of local Internet Service Providers (ISPs), many of them descended from the Bulletin Board Systems I'd covered in a book three years before.

The assumption was that FSN monopolies would control the Internet. My reporting showed this wasn't going to be the case. CMP re-launched *Interactive Age* as an Internet equipment publication in early 1995, and it went out of business by summer. It lost its original advertisers, and there were not enough Internet advertisers to sustain it.

## AT&T AND DSL

By this time, the analog Bell System I'd grown up with was dead.

It was killed by two forces, the political desire for competition and AT&T's desire to make more money catering to it.

The beginning of the end was the birth of a small company called Microwave Communication Inc. (MCI) in 1963.[215] MCI used microwave relay antennae to bypass AT&T's long-distance monopoly. Under William McGowan, it won a license to operate its network in competition with AT&T in 1969 and began a long antitrust battle to operate against the Bell System.

The Justice Department had first filed an antitrust suit against the Bell System in 1974 [216] but in 1982 AT&T agreed to break itself up, less because it understood the error of its ways than out of a desire to make more money for shareholders.

Under the agreement seven regional Bell companies were formed, each with a monopoly over basic telephone service in its own area.[217] Separate companies were spun out as Lucent, which would make telephone equipment, AT&T Communications, which inherited the AT&T name and operated the long-distance service, and NCR, whose acquisition as a computer subsidiary had proved a mistake. (NCR is now based in Atlanta and is in the business of credit and bank card transaction processing.)

This was still part of the status quo when I joined *Interactive Age*. Baby Bells like BellSouth were talking up a digital system for copper they called the Integrated Services Digital Network (ISDN). [218] Instead of sending analog signals over the local network. ISDN sent digital signals, using as much bandwidth as the thin copper lines could handle.

But let's back up for a moment. Because something had happened which foreshadowed AT&T's eventual demise. And I'd seen it first hand.

During the 1980s, companies like Hayes Microcomputer Products, based outside Atlanta, made a lot of money-making modulator-

215 MCI ads seemed ubiquitous in the 1970s. https://en.wikipedia.org/wiki/MCI_Communications

216 The case went almost unnoticed until the Bell System lost. https://en.wikipedia.org/wiki/Breakup_of_the_Bell_System

217 The break-up, and later reconstruction, of the Bell System were two of the biggest stories of my early journalism career. https://en.wikipedia.org/wiki/Breakup_of_the_Bell_System

218 ISDN was almost a thing. https://en.wikipedia.org/wiki/Integrated_Services_Digital_Network

demodulators (modems), which used part of the phone wire's bandwidth for digital data. Modem speeds quickly increased. My first modem, which I bought in 1982, ran at 300 bits/second, but was an improvement over the acoustic couplers running at 120 bits/second that preceded it.

Within a few years Hayes had 1,200 baud modems, then 2,400, and by the end of the decade it was selling 56,000 baud modems. It was at that time that founder Dennis Hayes, remembering me from my work at the *Atlanta Business Chronicle* in 1982, invited me to dinner and described his next big idea, a product BellSouth would sell that would make the entire phone network digital under the ISDN standard.

Hayes built thousands of Hayes ISDN modems, and waited for BellSouth to flip the switch on ISDN. He waited, and waited, and waited. Within a few years Hayes went out of business.

ISDN and Digital Subscriber Line (DSL), which simplified ISDN into a single digital signal, combined a Digital Signal Processor (remember them) on one end of a copper phone line with a digital modem on the other end. These would eventually enable you to run data at 1.5 Mbps, enough to transmit a basic television signal on a phone line.

Unfortunately for the Bells, the speed of DSL was ridiculous by the 1990s when compared with cable's Data Over Cable Service Interface Specification (DOCSIS).[219]

I contributed some chapters to a book about DOCSIS for cable operators around the time I left CMP in 1997. DOCSIS combined fiber rings between neighborhoods and existing coaxial cable. Coax, which was designed for TV, could carry more different frequencies than the Bells' copper. DOCSIS also let cable operators expand their capacity gradually, adding fiber the way a tree extends its branches.

The Bells never had a chance. By 2010 the old phone system was dying.

---

219 I wrote a few chapters as a freelancer. https://en.wikipedia.org/wiki/DOCSIS

# The Second AT&T

Once the ink was dried on their breakup, the former "Baby Bells" began plotting to get back together. The long-distance service began operating data services. Four of the babies eventually merged under the name SBC Communications, two others as Verizon, and the seventh became Qwest.

Mobile phones were treated as a competitive environment, with one license in each market given to the local Baby Bell, and one given over to a competitive bidder. Craig McCaw consolidated many of these competitive bidders into a company called McCaw Cellular, doing business as Cellular One. Then in 1994, the same year I joined *Interactive Age*, McCaw sold the company to the AT&T long distance company [220] for $12.6 billion.

This transaction saved AT&T, whose long-distance service was about to be overwhelmed by the Internet, and whose TV offerings would be beaten by cable. The new AT&T would be a cellular telephony network.

The old regional Bells at this time still had their half of the wireless business, and the opportunity to use their control of telephone poles to compete directly with the cable operators by adding fiber to their networks. But the change would take time, and money. To get that money, the regional Bells kept merging with one another, putting their capital into DSL.

SBC, which had been the regional Bell for Texas, Oklahoma, and St. Louis, merged with Ameritech, the regional Bell for the Midwest, in 1998. The merged company bought AT&T in 2005, taking its name, then acquired BellSouth in 2006 for $67 billion, along with its Cingular wireless service.

Having figured out that DSL wasn't competitive with DOCSIS, the promise of these later combinations was that the wired network would eventually be upgraded with fiber cable going right to subscribers' homes. Verizon called its fiber operation FiOS, eventually adding the old

---

220    This was the smartest deal AT&T ever made. https://en.wikipedia.org/wiki/AT%26T_Wireless_Services#McCaw_Cellular

GTE network in California and Florida to its holdings. AT&T called its fiber service U-Verse. Verizon, which had financed its wireless growth as a joint venture with Britain's Vodafone, finally bought out its partner in 2013 for $130 billion.

When Randall Stephenson became the new AT&T's CEO in 2013, after 12 years as a top executive, he saw a company with one-third of the wireless market, with a big chunk of the cable business, but not much respect from Wall Street because wired services were dying. The value of the company was barely half what it was at its peak in 2000, because of the debt being used for fiber.

Then he made what may have been a fatal mistake.

## AT&T Rejects the Cloud

By the time he became CEO, Stephenson had already seen Google develop the technologies that became known as the cloud. He saw Amazon doing the same thing. But he also saw the cost, a commitment of capital that began at $1 billion per quarter, as ruinous and held back. Even after Facebook, then a tiny fraction of AT&T's size, committed to building what are now called "cloud data centers" and launched an open source project called Open Compute to cut its construction costs, he held back.

Within a year of launching its cloud effort, in 2012, Facebook went public with a valuation of over $100 billion. In 2019 Facebook is worth twice what AT&T is worth. By 2021 it was worth four times AT&T.

Instead of investing in the cloud, the "core" of the Internet, Stephenson chose to invest at the network edge, where AT&T was already dominant. He put more money into U-Verse. Then he bought DirecTv for $67 billion in 2015.

Instead of confronting companies like Google and Amazon in the cloud, or even Microsoft, which committed to it in 2014 under new CEO Satya Nadella, Stephenson talked about the "edge cloud," [221] a set

---

221    This was another AT&T buzzword that, like ISDN, never took off because

of data centers between the clouds and local customers. This was a good business, an industry that by 2019 was worth over $100 billion with players such as Equinix, Digital Realty Trust, CoreSite and CyrusOne.

Unfortunately, Stephenson's talk about the "edge cloud" was mostly talk. Remember, Bell System founder Theodore Vail had also invented the concept of public relations. AT&T sold its managed data business to IBM in 2015[222] and its database customers to Oracle in 2017.[223] By 2019 AT&T was no longer a technology company. It sold technology, but as an agent for IBM.[224]

## AT&T BECOMES A CONTENT COMPANY

Instead of turning to the cloud, Stephenson sought to gain monopoly profits at the network edge.

AT&T decided to become a content company.

AT&T placed "data caps" on its wireless service, limiting video downloads unless it was paid for the extra bits. It planned to do the same thing for wired service. But data services were becoming so cheap that competitive pressures were making these caps irrelevant.

Meanwhile, the rise of Netflix, Google's YouTube and Amazon Prime began hitting U-Verse. The number of cable customers who "cut the cord," relying entirely on the Internet to deliver their entertainment, began rising steadily.[225] Some chose Internet entertainment from services like AT&T's own DirecTv Now.

AT&T didn't invest in it. https://about.att.com/ecms/dam/innovationdocs/Edge_Compute_White_Paper%20FINAL2.pdf

222     AT&T likes to claim it sells cloud. But it sells other peoples' cloud https://www.sdxcentral.com/articles/news/att-hands-managed-services-to-ibm-cloud/2015/12/

223     This is a story on the Oracle sale https://www.sdxcentral.com/articles/news/oracle-to-migrate-att-databases-to-cloud-platform/2017/05/

224     CNBC story got this story right https://www.cnbc.com/2019/07/16/ibm-signs-new-cloud-deal-with-att.html

225     Here are statistics on that from DigitalTrends https://www.digitaltrends.com/home-theater/cord-cutting-nielsen-2018/

AT&T's answer to the cord-cutting phenomenon was to become a content company. It doubled down on the cable model by announcing in 2017 it would buy Time Warner, owner of HBO, CNN, and other cable programming services, as well as the Warner Brothers movie studio, for $84 billion. Most of this money was in the form of new debt. It closed the deal in 2019.

In 2019 the AT&T phone network was essentially dead, the U-Verse cable service was being given the AT&T name and dying, while the AT&T Wireless service was being sped up by 5G so it might participate in cable's destruction. Amazon, SpaceX and OneWeb, meanwhile, were planning their constellations of low-Earth orbit satellites, controlled by cloud-based data centers and capable of delivering wireless services, at TV speeds, to everyone on the planet by the mid-2020s. By 2021 SpaceX had already launched hundreds of satellites and was telling people it would deliver Internet everywhere on the planet by the end of the year.

After buying DirecTv and Time Warner, and after forsaking the cloud, AT&T in July 2019 had $167 billion in actual debt, and tens of billions more in "technology debt." These were the hardware, software and systems that were, or were fast becoming, obsolete. With the number of streaming competitors growing by the day, and with customers having only a limited amount of time to watch it all, AT&T faced a bleak future.

In September 2019 Elliott Management, a hedge fund known for taking over companies, extracting profits and then leaving, took a stake in AT&T and claimed it could fix everything by selling a few peripheral units and introducing more focused management. Elliott wound up divesting its AT&T interest in 2020. [226]

Elliott knew something, however.

First, AT&T wound up being an enormous bidder in the late 2020 auction of so-called "C-Band" licenses for 5G service. Although AT&T already had a lot of spectrum, it hoped its $23.4 billion in new spectrum

226    Elliott's divestment story was covered by Fierce Wireless at https://www.
fiercewireless.com/operators/after-shaking-up-at-t-elliott-management-divests-its-
stake

(for which it would have to borrow $14 billion, [227] would let it dominate new Machine Internet services alongside long-time rival Verizon Wireless.

But where would it get the money?

In February 2021, AT&T announced it would divest its DirecTv and U-Verse cable businesses to private equity, valuing it at one-third of what the company had once paid for DirecTv alone. AT&T shareholders would retain about 70% of the resulting company, the private equity partners only 30%, but AT&T management would be out. [228]

A month later, AT&T announced it would sell its WarnerMedia content businesses in much the same way. In this case the partner was another public company, Discovery, which owned several cable channels and a streaming platform. The new company, called Warner-Discovery, will be 71% owned by AT&T shareholders, 29% by Discovery, but Discovery will operate it. [229]

The only hope for the new AT&T, in other words, is that Moore's Law of Radios will save it. But will it?

227    From Fierce Wireless, a grade paper. https://www.fiercewireless.com/financial/at-t-looks-to-borrow-14b-for-5g-spectrum-report
228    CNBC covered the story at https://www.cnbc.com/2021/02/25/att-to-spin-off-directv-att-tv-now-and-u-verse-into-new-company.html
229    The Washington Post covered the Warner-Discovery deal https://www.washingtonpost.com/business/2021/05/22/discovery-warner-media-att-spinoff/

# Chapter 9

# Moore's Law of Software

Software is the most valuable product we have that's still mostly handmade.

Hardware depends entirely on software. Software is essential to the productivity gains of Moore's Law.

The enormous productivity gains of Moore's Law are thus dependent on something that must be made entirely by hand.


## Moore's Law of Software Development

Moore's Law of Software Development is that there is no Moore's Law of Software Development.

This lesson was being learned around the same time Gordon Moore wrote his famous article. It was described in Frederick Brook's classic *The Mythical Man-Month.* [230]

Brooks wrote his book after leading a vast team of programmers working to develop the IBM S/360 computer, which was introduced I 1964.[231]

The software for the S/360 nearly destroyed IBM. As then-IBM chairman Thomas Watson Jr. explained in his own memoir, called *Father, Son & Co.,*[232] the more people he assigned to the project, the further behind it got. The expense and the tensions this caused kept Watson's beloved brother Dick from succeeding him as head of the

230 I was fortunate enough to meet Mr. Brooks at the 2019 Heidelberg Laureate conference. https://en.wikipedia.org/wiki/The_Mythical_Man-Month
231 This is Wikipedia's page on the S/360. https://en.wikipedia.org/wiki/IBM_System/360
232     For Mr. Watson this was one of the saddest chapters in his life. https://www.amazon.com/dp/B00DXKJ6KE/

company, because Dick accepted blame for the delays.

As Watson Jr. learned to his horror and as Brooks described in his book, people write and test code at a fixed rate. As more people are added to a project they must be trained and coordinate with one another to stay on task. Worse, programmers are human. Key programmers get sick or go on vacation. As the number of people involved in a project rises, productivity per programmer goes down.

This has been the case throughout my wife's career as a programmer. It's a lot more difficult to coordinate software development than to code. It takes more talent to define software than to write it. English is the most important programming language there is.

The pressure of deadlines, the necessity for overtime, and the need to be conversant with the latest programming tools, have all combined to make programming at the leading edge in Silicon Valley a young person's game. Just as reporters quickly become editors, columnists, or public relations people, so coders quickly become managers or systems analysts.

Many techniques have been tried to reduce the burdens inherent in Moore's Law of Software Development.

One is to break projects into many pieces, which increases coordination costs but makes it possible to recover from a single programmer's mistakes or life situation.

Or the work can be redesigned, as in Agile development [233], where quick-and-dirty, barely functional core software is prioritized and everything else is added on later.

Because there is no Moore's Law of Software Development, Silicon Valley quickly crafted a new workstyle that reminded observers of life on a college campus. People would work extra-long weeks, sometimes for months at a time, to complete a project, living on soda, candy, and adrenaline. Then they might take off several months to recover from it. It's not a healthy way to live, but in this case it works.

---

233     Here is Wikipedia on Agile. https://en.wikipedia.org/wiki/Agile_software_development

This is what many of us did in college. We would party until deadlines neared, then pull "all-nighters" to get the work done. Once the work was done there came a period of decompression, a "summer vacation." In the case of software developers, the length of this break is driven by the pressure placed on the worker during the project. Even if they come back to the job quickly, they're usually given other tasks between projects.

You can still see this ethos at companies like Google. The workspace is designed for 24-7 use, with places set aside as virtual playpens, and provision made for people to sleep at the office when necessary.

There's a second model for this, however, which harkens back to the pre-Industrial Revolution. Since software is made by hand, why not make it at home?

Many programmers have long lived at home, but the 2020 COVID-19 pandemic accelerated the move. Companies were forced to rely on at-home workforces to build and maintain their software. To their surprise, it worked. The companies saved money, the workers saved both money and time, while new tools like Zoom Video and Slack, which hadn't existed a decade before, kept everyone together. As the pandemic was ebbing in 2021 many companies were telling workers to return to the office, but how many will want to lose those savings?

## Portable, Compatible Software

The S/360, which came out a year after Gordon Moore's famous essay, did accomplish one great thing. It made Moore's Law of Software possible.

That's because the S/360 was built with an Operating System, code that defined how the computer would react to any type of job, and which worked across the product line. Once you programmed a System/360, the software you wrote would run on any other System/360. It was "portable." The only limits on application portability were those imposed by the hardware.

This is the key to everything that has happened in computing since. A single stable operating system makes software portable. While it's true that, as Brooks wrote later in *The Mythical Man-Month*, there is "No Silver Bullet" to the organizational challenges of software development, there are ways to improve programmer productivity.

Still operating systems, and hardware innovations that came after, did finally make the power of software increase in line with Moore's Law. They used what I call Moore's Law of Software.

## Moore's Law of Software:

### Software's power increases with its distribution

Once a program is written and works, it should run again. Once a program is written and works, it becomes portable. You can copy it onto another computer of the same type, and it will run. Bugs will be found, maintenance may have to be performed, copying can create errors, but once the program is done and runs, the only costs of running it again are the costs of maintenance. The only costs of bringing it to market are the marginal costs of marketing and distribution.

If you design and build a car or a plane based on plans, there is still an enormous marginal cost in building another one. But if you design and build a software product, there should be little or no marginal cost in running the program on another computer, save the cost of getting it onto that computer.

Moore's Law has since dropped the marginal cost of getting software onto computers to zero. Moore's Law of Hardware made Moore's Law of Software possible.

## The 1970s: The Age of Unix

It cost IBM an enormous amount of money to develop the S/360. It took an enormous effort to sell it, and more money to maintain it, fixing bugs and developing enhancements.

Despite Moore's Law of Software, software has never been 100% reliable. To reduce its liability, IBM didn't sell its software. It licensed it, writing contracts that let customers use the software, but maintaining IBM's ownership and control of the underlying code. You had to buy the S/360, at IBM's price, to run the S/360 operating system. IBM also sold training, maintenance, and applications written for specific industries. This was an illegal monopoly.

Under pressure from the government IBM separated hardware sales from software in 1968.

The software industry was born.

The S/360 that was announced in 1964 but delivered two years later was a single-computer operating system. Programmers were quick to come up with the demand for a multi-computer operating system. One such project, sponsored by AT&T's Bell Labs, and conducted at MIT with help from General Electric, was called Multiplexed Information and Computing Service (Multics). Multics, which was under development through the late 1960s, would let several people use a computer simultaneously, even from remote terminals.

Unix, now the most popular operating system in the world, was based on Multics. It was designed to create competition for the IBM mainframes, the S/360 and its successors, but was originally designed as a single-user system. It was written by a team at Bell Labs headed by Ken Thompson and Dennis Ritchie. It was smaller and simpler than Multics and could perform only one task at a time. But it included many Multics concepts, like a hierarchical file system, the concepts of computer processes and device files, and a command line interpreter. By August 1969, the Thompson-Ritchie team was able to produce a self-hosting operating system built on a GE-Honeywell computer. [234] The name Unix is a pun on Multics.

During the early 1970s many versions of Unix were developed, although portability suffered as vendors added their own tweaks for corporate advantage. This was the golden age of the minicomputer, building Massachusetts companies like Digital Equipment, Data

234 Computer programmers love puns. As Wikipedia describes it, this is one of their best. https://en.wikipedia.org/wiki/History_of_Unix

General, and Wang Labs. Each had its own version of the Unix operating system, and its own software "stack" of applications and utilities.[235] But the computers were only the size of refrigerators, and you could hide them in a closet rather than building a special room for them. You could also run wires around the office for terminals so most of the workforce could access the resource.

Still, the various versions or "flavors" of Unix, and the competition created by having many small, nimble companies making Unix computers, did drop the costs of using computer operating systems.

## The 1980s: The Age of Shrink-wrap

Software was added to the copyright law by Congress in 1980. [236]

This brought about the age of "shrink-wrap" software, software people felt they were buying because it came on a disk from a store. But, like IBM's software before it, this software was technically only licensed for use on a single machine by a single person.

By this time, of course, Moore's Law had been spinning for almost 15 years, chip technology defining what computers could do, and how fast they could do it. The movie industry moved to California in the 1910s to get away from Thomas Edison's intellectual property. The software industry moved to California in the 1970s to get closer to the semiconductor industry's patents and copyrights. The software giants of Silicon Valley were thus based around hardware companies like Intel, Apple, and Hewlett-Packard. By working closely with chip companies like Intel, software companies could assure that their programs ran on the latest computers.

As hardware improved, software became capable of handling more complicated files, and more simply. But it was still, fundamentally, the same industry as in the 1960s. Whether the software came on a floppy

235 The best book about designing computers during this period remains Tracy Kidder's book, *The Soul of a New Machine*. You can still get it at Amazon. https://www.amazon.com/Soul-New-Machine-Tracy-Kidder/dp/0316491977 Just realize that it's now a history book.
236 Here is the relevant law. https://uscode.house.gov/view.xhtml?req=granuleid:USC-prelim-title17-section101&num=0&edition=prelim

disk, CD or DVD, whether the code represented a program, a collection of songs, or a movie, you were still buying a license, not a real product. There was still a cost to creating the media, packaging it along with a manual, stocking shelves, then installing it.

The nature of shrink-wrap software changed only slightly after Microsoft released Windows 3.0 in 1990 and made it possible to mass-market software that needed more than 640 Kilobytes of memory to run, an architectural limit built into early IBM PCs.[237] The breaching of the barrier brought a host of "multimedia" applications to the market, which included graphics files, sound files, and video files accessible by software. This meant that software itself moved from floppies to CDs to DVDs.

But it was still the same business, with the same business model as before.

## THE 1990S: THE RISE OF THE INTERNET

I can date the turn of the software business precisely.

It came in November 1994, at the annual Comdex show in Las Vegas, which had become the primary site for technology announcements because it had the largest convention center.

This was the year Hollywood came to Comdex. A host of stars, including Quincy Jones, Linda Ronstadt, and "Roger Rabbit" voice actor Charles Fleischer, all of whom I met that night, came up to celebrate the launch of a new DVD from a start-up called 7th Level, which many Hollywood types were backing.

The disk was called *Tuneland*. As noted in Chapter 3, it was voiced by comedian-actor Howie Mandel. It was a cartoon-based learning game. All schools needed do to run it was to replace their hardware with machines that could run Windows 95, costing just a few thousand dollars each.

---

237 There's conventional memory and expanded memory, not unconventional memory. https://en.wikipedia.org/wiki/Conventional_memory

My kids were young then. After returning from Comdex, I spent the money. They thought the software was cool.

I had just taken my job with *Interactive Age*. The Web was just starting to happen. Editor David Klein sat in his office with a T-1 line, running at the then unheard-of speed of 1.5 megabits/second, saying he "had fire" because he now understood the future.

The Internet was the future.

At the 7th Level party, I was standing by Mr. Fleischer when a fan turned up. Not a fan of Mr. Fleischer. Of me. The *Interactive Age Daily* was, unknown to me, drawing an enormous (for the time) audience of 10,000 readers per day.

I introduced the fan to Mr. Fleischer, who didn't recognize him, and it was then that I realized the world had changed. Within a year, the whole world of manufacturing, distribution, and retail that 7th Level had been built to support collapsed, replaced by the Internet model.

The Internet model turbocharged Moore's Law of Software because it dropped the marginal cost for software distribution. Companies that had spent millions to sell thousands of shrink-wrapped software packages now found they could put that software on a Web site and distribute millions of copies in days.

The Internet also represented a new beginning for software. Shrink-wrapped software had been getting bigger-and-bigger with time, increasing the cost to maintain it. On the Internet, tiny programs became vital again. Early Internet ads were tiny billboards. Games that hadn't been played for 20 years came online and drew traffic that could be monetized with ads.

With software having zero marginal cost to distribute (and with word of mouse helping to market it), business models changed. Instead of selling software, it was now profitable to give it away and support it with advertising.

New types of large-scale software also developed. A host of new "search engines" appeared to help users get where they wanted to go, with names like Excite, Yahoo, Ask Jeeves and Altavista. These were designed to help people find Web sites, and made magazines like *Interactive Age* (or *NetGuide*, to which I was moved a year later) obsolete. Within two decades search engines would make even magazines obsolete, and many other industries.

Many Wall Street analysts treated the Internet as a new medium, like print or TV, and told the new Internet entrepreneurs they needed to expand, becoming "portals" with news, entertainment, and free Web pages. The companies that listened to Wall Street, like Yahoo, quickly failed.

That's because the Internet wasn't a new medium. It was, in my words, an "extra-large." The Internet wasn't just an advertising medium. Entire businesses could be built on the Internet, doing everything from prospecting for customers to selling goods and services, and supporting those sales.

This seemed obvious to Jeff Bezos, who launched Amazon.Com as an online bookstore in 1994. The idea of focusing on search seemed obvious to Sergey Brin and Larry Page, who launched Google four years later.

## THE 2000s: THE DECADE OF OPEN SOURCE

When I wrote the first edition of this book, in 2002, and even when I updated it in 2010, I said open source was the greatest force for programmer productivity since the PC.

Open source spreads software development costs over a theoretically unlimited number of people and companies. An open source program's code is visible to everyone, not closed the way proprietary systems like Microsoft Windows or Apple's MacOS were. Users can download it free, fix it themselves, add to it, and (depending on the conditions on the software, contained in a license agreement) profit from their work on it.

The most important open source program is the Linux operating system. Linux is a version of Unix, software that was already decades-old when programmer Linus Torvalds, then a 21-year old Finnish computer programming student, wrote the first version of his kernel in 1991.[238] (The name Linux is a mash-up of his first name and Unix.)

Linux took off in 1992 after a graphical user interface (like that of Microsoft Windows) was adapted to it. In that year Torvalds also began licensing it under the General Public License.

This brings us to licensing agreements.

Free and Open Source Software (FOSS)[239] is based on a movement created in the 1980s by programmer Richard Stallman.[240] It was a reaction to the rise of Microsoft and its "End User License Agreements" or EULAs. https://en.wikipedia.org/wiki/End-user_license_agreement

Under a EULA contract, the company that writes the software doesn't really sell it. It just "licenses" it. The customer can't see the software and the company "selling" it won't even guarantee it will work. Customers only buy the right to use code on a specific machine.

IBM had licensed software in this way since before the S/360. It was adapted to the shrink-wrap era by Microsoft, which licensed its MS-DOS program to IBM for the PC.

But the PC age made explicit something that looked unfair to Stallman, long known by the initials RMS. After all, you hand someone money, they hand you a disk, yet you don't really own what's on the disk? By 1990 Microsoft was selling millions of disks in this way, while retaining the same control over software that IBM had used to keep mainframe customers from bolting to rivals in the 1950s.

Stallman's ideas were codified in a General Public License (GPL),[241] which Torvalds adopted for his software. The name GNU means "GNU's

238     Wikipedia has a history of Linux, possibly the most important program in the world. https://en.wikipedia.org/wiki/History_of_Linux
239     Wikipedia's page on FOSS https://en.wikipedia.org/wiki/Free_Software_Foundation
240     Stallman had great ideas but was also a jerk, which eventually cost him his position and may, in 2021, destroy the FSF itself. Wikipedia keeps its Stallman page updated. https://en.wikipedia.org/wiki/Richard_Stallman
241     Wikipedia's page on the GPL. https://en.wikipedia.org/wiki/GNU_General_Public_License

Not Unix." It was Stallman who called the movement Free and Open Source Software (FOSS).

The GPL explicitly gave users four freedoms:

1. The freedom to see the code
2. The freedom to change the code,
3. The freedom to share the code, and
4. The freedom to gain access to improvements on the code.

The freedom to see the code started the open source revolution.

It was the last freedom – the freedom to see others' improvements – that split Stallman from what became open source. Stallman called his process CopyLeft. Instead of copyright giving all rights to the programmer, CopyLeft licenses like the GPL gave all rights to the user.

The open source movement developed in the late 1990s as a response to FOSS among programmers who wanted to profit from code, even while it was visible. Many of the ideas behind this movement are encapsulated in a book by Eric Raymond called *The Cathedral and the Bazaar*.[242]

While approving the idea of visible code, Raymond and his followers objected to Stallman's fourth freedom, the freedom to gain access to improvements. They said this last freedom imprisoned programmers, forcing them to give away all work. The new licenses arising from this are sometimes called permissive licenses, because they give software writers permission to profit. The difference between FOSS and open source is that an open source programmer may keep some enhancements to himself and profit from them.

Many open source licenses evolved from this understanding. Among

---

242    Raymond's book remains a classic. Here is its Wikipedia page. https://en.wikipedia.org/wiki/The_Cathedral_and_the_Bazaar

the first to emerge was the Berkeley Standard Development License (BSD), created at the University of California at Berkeley. [243] These licenses maintain the first three freedoms of code but allow those who download tools to sell improvements.

Among the first big projects developed under these new licenses was Eclipse[244], a collection of software authoring tools which sponsors, now including IBM, enhanced, and sold, as well as the Apache [245] projects, which began with a Web server but now includes many other tools under the same license and foundation structure. Linus Torvald's Linux also has a foundation behind it, called the Linux Foundation.[246] Corporations support the foundations with money and people, but individuals are always welcome to join and contribute.

Most people will never view the open source code they download. But consumers can still contribute to projects by testing early versions of the code and reporting bugs, a process called beta testing. (The foundations also take cash.)

During the 2000s open source programs like Linux, Apache and Eclipse began providing stiff competition to Microsoft applications, especially in the enterprise market. By this time, every large company had its own programming staff, its own computing department, and these people liked that open source let them maintain control of the company codebase.

Microsoft's initial response was a new policy on intellectual property. It's described in the book *Burning the Ships*[247] by Marshall Phelps, its chief intellectual property lawyer during the middle of the decade.

Where Microsoft previously made business partners sign agreements

---

243     Here is how Wikipedia describes BSD licensing. https://en.wikipedia.org/wiki/BSD_licenses
244     The Eclipse Foundation is online at http://www.eclipse.org/
245     I once spoke at an Apache conference. Here is their home page http://www.apache.org/
246     The Linux Foundation's importance has only grown with time. Here is their home page. https://www.linuxfoundation.org/
247     I still have my copy of this book. It's good. https://www.amazon.com/Burning-Ships-Intellectual-Transformation-Microsoft/dp/0470432152/

not to assert patent rights against its code, Microsoft under Phelps began aggressively patenting elements of its code and using those rights to force its way into the open source market. This was a rear-guard action, although it worked for a while.

The biggest impact of open source, however, turned out to be very bad for people who tried to make a business out of it.

That's because, by design, the bulk of open source's value goes to the users of software. It doesn't go to the developer. That's in the license, even a "permissive" license. Most companies created to profit from selling support for open source projects didn't do well, or not nearly as well as their investors expected. Most corporate users could support open source themselves.

To developers of new software tools this sounds unfair. It shouldn't. Jim Whitehurst, CEO of open source developer Red Hat, now part of IBM, explained it to me. Open source is the equivalent of standard wrenches, bolts, and screws, doing what the new machine shops did in the early 19th century, two generations into the Industrial Revolution. (When he told me this, computing itself was about 60 years old.)

It was standardized tools, parts, and processes that made possible the great trains, planes, and airplanes for which the Industrial Revolution is known. Mass produced bolts, fasteners and tools were a necessary first step toward the greater revolution, in the same way that standard, open source tools are a necessary first step the scaled systems that will come out of our time.

While it seems reasonable that Boeing and General Motors are worth more than Black & Decker, even though standard tools were necessary for their success, this doesn't make the owners of today's toolmakers feel any better. So, in the late 2010s attempts have been made to amend the open source agreement with software called "Open Core." Open Core software claims to be open source but gives control of enhancements to the company that made the original tool. Another way in which programmers try to get paid for code is what they call an "open core" model. [248] The idea is that feature-limited versions are

248    The term dates from 2008 but in 2021 Wikipedia still said there were multiple issues with its article on it https://en.wikipedia.org/wiki/Open-core_model,

available as open source, but enhancements are made proprietary.

Once Microsoft began adapting to open source there remained one big company (besides IBM, whose influence was already fading) upholding the proprietary banner, Oracle. Oracle bought Sun Microsystems in 2010 and, with it, control of key open source technologies like Java, the Solaris operating system, and the Open Office suite. It asserted copyright on the Application Program Interfaces (APIs) used to explain how the tools worked.

Oracle won an important legal victory over Google in 2018 [249]. A federal appeals court ruled that Google's method for implementing Java for its Android phones violated the Oracle copyrights. In early 2021 the Supreme Court overrode the Appeals Court, ruling that Google's use of the Oracle's API was "Fair Use." It did not rule on whether APIs can be copyrighted.

The assertion of copyright, with an aim to gain control of the underlying open source code, remains a threat to the open source movement as this is written. Most important tools are now held by private foundations, like Eclipse or Apache, but the story is not yet ended. Whether the advances open source brought to software will be fully realized in the next decade is also up in the air.

While open source has not proven to be the "silver bullet" that would let programmer productivity to grow in line with Moore's Law, it has delivered enormous productivity. Open source fosters re-use of code, it enables competitors to work together, and it enables collaboration between those who create code and companies that use it. In 2021 it is the dominant mode of enterprise software development.

Open source creates a high and constantly rising platform for new software development. Programmers no longer need to start with a blank sheet of paper. They can build with standard parts, at minimal cost. Combined with the Internet's dropping of distribution and marketing costs to zero, open source had put Moore's Law into overdrive by 2010.

---

a testament to its controversial nature.

249     Here is Wikipedia's page on Google vs. Oracle https://en.wikipedia.org/wiki/Google_LLC_v._Oracle_America,_Inc.

# The 2010s: Cloud and Devices

One event and a long-term trend upended the old order after 2010 and let software take over the world.

The event was the 2007 MacWorld show, when Apple CEO Steve Jobs introduced the iPhone and launched the "device" era.

The iPhone, and the competing Android devices that followed it, revolutionized software in two ways. First, it once again gave them a blank sheet of paper for development. More important it brought software distribution out from behind the desk, into the street.

That's because the iPhone isn't a phone. It's an Internet client. Compared to what had been available when I began my career, it's a networked supercomputer you hold in your hand and put in your pocket.

The iPhone eliminated user training. It also got rid of my work in computer journalism, because "apps" could be downloaded in moments and their use was intuitive.

The evolution was called the Cloud.

To help their search engine scale to billions of users, Google combined a virtual operating system, sitting on top of any program, with distributed computing model that developed in the 1990s that let work be split among several computers. To this it added open source software, along with commodity hardware and a rigorous focus on costs, including re-use of the energy given off by its systems.

The result was a new kind of computing, infinitely scalable and instantly accessible. The cloud was developed in the middle of the 2000s but came to define the 2010s.

As soon as Amazon.Com began building cloud infrastructure for its own online store, its management understood something Google had missed. Amazon saw that it could rent out its cloud, just as it was renting its warehousing and distribution infrastructure, to other companies. This would bring it the capital it needed to make the cloud bigger.

By 2010[250] Amazon Web Services was the most valuable piece of the company, and Amazon was building a network of "hyperscale" data centers around the world to spread its benefits.

This turned out to be just the first chapter in the cloud story.

In 2021 Amazon is no longer alone using the cloud model. Microsoft transformed itself to support it with the Azure Cloud starting early in the 2010s. Apple eventually built its Apple Cloud. Google, now called Alphabet, began selling its services as the Google Cloud and, since 2018, has been very aggressive in seeking markets for it.

The most remarkable cloud story may be that of Facebook, which began building its own cloud network even before it had the $1 billion/quarter in cash flow needed to justify it. Over the last five years I have taken to calling these companies the "Cloud Czars." In 2021 they were worth a combined $7 billion. They are the world economy's landlords.

China quickly recognized the cloud, closed its market off from the Cloud Czars, and developed its own "Cloud Emperors" in Alibaba Group Holding, Tencent Holding and Baidu. Alibaba is the only one of these companies that is globally competitive. In 2021 it was bidding to be worth even more than Facebook.

Clouds and devices have brought the benefits of Moore's Law, and Moore's Law of Software, to the entire world. A farmer in Botswana can now be connected to the global conversation, and the global market. People in Ethiopia, Ghana, even in the remotest corners of India and Southeast Asia, can now develop and distribute their own apps to a global market.

This is the revolution that has transformed the world, and that frightens gatekeepers around the world. One billion people have been pulled out of poverty, in the 21st century, with the help of clouds, devices, and open source. They have homes, they can be educated, and they have hope for their children.

In the process, clouds and devices have also overturned every

---

250 This old "what's new" page was still being maintained in 2021. https://aws.amazon.com/about-aws/whats-new/2010/

industry. My own job as a computer journalist is just one casualty.

Clouds and devices brought a new term to the vocabulary of computing. Disruption. Disruption can turn any industry upside-down in what appears a moment, destroying careers, lifetimes, and entire professions.

As I described in Chapter 8, clouds and devices have eliminated the telephone industry. They have destroyed what was once the journalism industry. They have turned the entire media industry on its head and created a "Retail Armageddon" for anyone who can't compete with Amazon's economics, even in the remotest country towns.

In the last 10 years clouds and devices have unemployed real estate agents, bankers, insurance agents, and taxi drivers. Anything that was organized can be re-organized by an app, distributed in a cloud, with buyers and sellers negotiating prices directly. There seems to be no end to disruption.

There is still no Moore's Law of Software Development, but Moore's Law of Software has given technology power over the whole economy, on a global scale.

While I have written about software for most of my life, I can't write it. I tried to do it at Rice. I tried again in the 1990s, and again in the 2000s. I make misteaks. I have trouble finding them. (Can you help?) Code needs to be absolutely, positively 100% accurate to run. This paragraph isn't.

But there's hope.

## The Most Important Programming Language

I didn't learn the most important point about software until after I wrote the first edition of this book.

My dear wife taught me.

My wife became a computer programmer in 1981. In 1983

she took her present job. Over two decades she learned Assembly Language, she had learned COBOL, she mastered the secrets of SQL databases and spreadsheets. But in the middle of the 2000s her career was going nowhere, because like me she preferred doing her job to managing others who did it.

That's when her employer made a fateful, expensive, but essential decision. They decided to replace the mainframes she had been working on with a client-server network.

Before it could create the new system, however, my wife's company would have to document every program running on their system. It was a huge task, and many people were assigned to it, each given a selection of programs to document. The documents would then be checked and edited by a committee of managers.

Since the authors of these instructions were programmers, not journalists, many of the documents the committee got were poorly written. But when my wife's documents came before the committee, I'm told there was an audible sigh of happiness around the table.

Not only could my wife write good English, but she could also describe what she had written in clear, simple sentences. When the committee learned this, her career took off.

Soon she had a new nickname at work. She was The Oracle. (No relation to the company.)

"I don't understand this requirement, what does it mean?" someone would ask. "You'll need to ask The Oracle," they would be told.

My wife went from documenting the existing system to writing, and organizing, requirements for the new system her company was creating. Once the new system was in place, she became a systems analyst, and while she never did become a manager, she is highly respected by her colleagues. She became an essential interface between the people running the business of her system and those doing the actual coding. She also makes more money than I ever dreamt of making from writing. [251]

While she still loves coding my wife has risen above it, into a higher calling, using the same tools I used in creating this book, the tools of journalism. Learning, taking careful notes, understanding what's important, and writing clearly.

That's where the hope lies for all those who, like me, lack the patience and precision to write software.

Bring the most important computing language with you, wherever you go, and you will go far.

No matter what you do in this world of the future it's the ability to learn, comprehend, and explain, in clear simple sentences, that will get you there.

---

251 At my first j-school lecture, the teacher told us that if we wanted to have a good living, we should find a spouse with a good job. I proposed marriage to my wife that day and have never regretted it.

# CHAPTER 10
# MOORE'S LAW OF POLITICS

Before Moore's Law kicked into gear, technologists were political conservatives.

Gordon Moore was a Republican. David Packard of Hewlett-Packard, the first great California tech company, was Deputy Secretary of Defense under Richard Nixon.

There were good reasons for this. Computer technology developed as a Cold War activity. Much of the research that brought us today's world was funded by the U.S. military.

Technology helped America win the war, and not just with the atomic bomb.

- The U.S. military found its experts through IBM punch card readers.

- Hedy Lamarr developed what became WiFi for the U.S. military, and it remained a secret until long after the patent expired.

- The first computer, ENIAC, was a military project, meant to create firing tables.

- The Apollo Program, from which software developed, was justified by the Cold War.

- The Internet was originally DARPANet, for Defense Advanced Research Project Agency Network.

Military research dollars let technologists do their work without worrying about money. It made them mission oriented. The model was Hewlett Packard, with its white shirts, thin ties, and 10 AM coffee breaks.

But as technology came to be at the center of society, this would change.

## CYCLES IN AMERICAN POLITICS

To understand this, let me briefly go back to America's beginnings.

Ever since Alexander Hamilton created America's financial system in the 1790s, the politics of America have been based largely on the needs of industry. Whichever industry provided the greatest additional value to the economy would end up calling the political tune. Until it didn't anymore, and a new, more valuable industry replaced it.

In other words, the business of America is business. If you want to know where politics is going, follow the money.

Simple machines like the cotton gin made slavery pay starting in the early 19th century. Slavery drove American politics for 60 years as a result. It was the snake under the bed during the Constitutional Convention, but the cotton gin made it into a dragon.

For me, the most important piece of fiction during this period was the story of John Henry, a black "steel driving man" who took on a machine in building a railroad, won, but immediately died of a heart attack. [252] The story held all the economic elements of the period together. The black man was enslaved by a difficult job, the machine could replace him, the railroad and its machine pointed the way ahead.

Railroads won the Civil War. When push came to shove, when the old economic model met the new, railroads' ability to move men and materiel to the front, and raw materials to factories, won the day. The late 19th century would be based on the needs of railroads. It was a battle for capital and a return on the investment. The Gilded Age was all about moving money around for the rail magnates, the economy's

---

252    I described this on my blog in 2011, as part of a personal study of political history. https://www.danablankenhorn.com/2011/05/john-henry-in-dilberts-cube.html

growing production funneled into a few hands.

By the 1890s it was becoming clear railroads weren't the only infrastructure inventors would need to create an urban society. America would also need electric utilities, transit utilities, a telephone utility. They would need to be utilities because manufacturers needed stable input prices to succeed. So did factories that would use the steel to make rail cars, automobiles, and airplanes.

The Progressive Era was built on providing this stability. A new economic order was established by bankers like J.P. Morgan, by magnates like John D. Rockefeller, and by executives like Theodore Vail of AT&T. Capital would be deployed at scale. The resulting monopolies would have their profits guaranteed, but regulated, allowing the manufacturers who were their customers to prosper.

The Great Depression proved that this new manufacturing machine also needed scaled demand to meet its scaled supply. The Depression was a deflationary spiral, prices falling, people being laid off in hope lower production would yield a profit, then prices falling again, and employment being cut again. Demand was required to meet the supply problem. New money, new programs, and new armies were the response. After World War II, acts like the Marshall Plan and the G.I. Bill allowed civilian as well as military demand to rise. This was the golden age of manufacturing. Mass production met the mass consumption.

Gordon Moore grew to manhood during the age of manufacturing. Born in 1929, he was a child of the Great Depression and of World War II. He became an engineer against the backdrop of growing peacetime prosperity. There was a consensus among politicians in favor of both guns and butter, with arguments at the margins over how much and for whom.

It's said that what split this world apart was Vietnam. But there was an economic force under the surface. Even during the height of the manufacturing era, it could be seen in films like *Giant* and in the hotel suites of cities like Houston, where Lyndon Johnson played poker with oil equipment magnates George and Herman Brown. There was a new gating factor for growth, because manufacturing productivity only rose at a few percentage points per year and was swallowed up by wage growth.

The new gating factor was resources. It was access raw materials. It was oil. Maintaining prosperity meant maintaining access to this raw material.

Oil was becoming the engine of American growth even during the manufacturing era. Stories of oilmen in the 1950s would track closely with those of technologists a generation later. Oil was easy money. Cash came out of the ground.

When oil appeared to become scarce, in the 1970s, when it became clear that the richest deposits were outside the U.S., gaining control over those resources became key to keeping America great. Money was diverted from civilian to military use, as in Moore's youth, but this time the goal was strictly economic, control of the commodity that meant prosperity.

The resource politics of Reagan and the Bushes was great for the resource industries. But they weren't great for every American industry.

## THE TECHNOLOGY LIFESTYLE

The PC revolution of the 1970s began technology's march toward a new political order.

PCs let technology break beyond the engineering market, into the mass market. Moore's Law could create wealth even more effectively than control of oil could do it.

I saw this first in 1980, when I came home from my reporting job in Houston to find a neighbor had bought a networked computer and four terminals for about $20,000. This neighbor was hiring other people to transcribe court records on the terminals, which were sent to her via modem and printed. Courts were paying $1/page for the transcripts. She, and the women under her, were working from home.

A new generation of tech leaders, like Steve Jobs and Bill Gates, were teenagers during the war in Vietnam. They had no attachment to companies descended from military contractors, like Intel or Hewlett Packard. HP declined not to buy the longhairs' idea for a new computer called the Apple, much like Western Union turned down the Bell patents a century earlier. New software-based companies didn't have attachments to the oil industry, either, or to the military contracting system that tied technology to the government.

But they still faced *The Mythical Man Month.*

Their cure, as discussed in Chapter 9, was overtime. Coders would go into hyperdrive, fueled by coffee and candy bars, and meet impossible deadlines. Then they would crash, leaving the office for weeks or even months at a time, before gearing up for their next project.

The model for what an office should look like gradually shifted. The corporate campus became a college campus. A coder's workstyle became a lifestyle. Developers would stay at the office 24-7 during a push, playing games to stay sane, crashing at the office to recharge. [253]

Salesmen were not the stars at these new technology companies. Now, in what was increasingly called "Silicon Valley," developers were the stars. Developers gave salesmen something to sell. If some looked a little strange, if they were in at odd hours, that was fine. If they were women, if they were gay, if they were from another country, even if they were confined to a wheelchair, it didn't matter. Concepts mattered. Code mattered. Brains mattered.

The change was gradual. The mood at IBM and Hewlett Packard Comdex booths during the 1980s, when I started covering the field, was as grim as ever. I called their small hospitality rooms, where salesmen met prospects after the show closed, "hostility suites." Younger companies happily let reporters into their evening sales events, which I took to calling "food frenzies." We measured their success by the size and abundance of the free buffet shrimp, and the kind of alcohol they

---

253    The upheaval between the old attitudes in technology and the new were described best in the comic strip Dilbert, by Scott Adams. When Interactive Age was closed, our staff was able to invite a guest speaker for our company's annual dinner. We chose Scott, and he sat at our table. https://dilbert.com/

offered reporters at the open bar.

More important, the new system worked on the bottom line. Developers who hadn't cared for formalities rose to become executives who didn't care for formalities. Moore's Law of Software meant that, as distribution shifted from floppy disks and CDs to the Internet, developers were creating insane amounts of value.

Bill Gates was the avatar of the new style. In the 1990s he became the subject of what I called "Sam Walton" stories, meant to show what a regular guy he was. The most popular was of him and his number two, Steve Ballmer, flying First Class to Microsoft's Initial Public Offering, joking about the luxury and the bankers who had wasted their money on it. Gates also reportedly carried his own suit bag on business trips, and during the 1980s was insanely available during Comdex, where we would seek him out at the "secret Dvorak party," named for ZDNet columnist John Dvorak.

We were all young then.

## What Tech Learned

As tech companies scaled and matured in the 1990s and 2000s, driven by Moore's Law, their hunger for talent only grew, and their politics shifted. Their politics became centered on people.

Just as the Internet represented a tipping point for technology growth, so it represented the start of a change in America's politics. Class distinctions within technology were reduced. If you could do the job, you were needed. The "help wanted" sign was always out.

Tech companies didn't just need coders. They needed executives who could get the most from diverse workforces. They needed writers who could explain technology to investors, business partners, employees, the media, and the public. As software came to embrace mass manipulation of images, sound and video, technology companies came to need artists. As Apple products embraced cutting-edge design, the industry needed designers.

The search for such people became global. Promising executives were recruited from Taiwan, from India, and from Europe. Women began rising to prominence. The need for talent caused tech to start supporting gay rights. Even disability no longer mattered if the talent was there. Stephen Hawking was worth thousands of ordinary minds.

This shifted the politics of technology. California went to the Democrats in the mid-1990s and never went back. Other tech centers followed.

Writers like Richard Florida wrote, in his classic *The Rise of the Creative Class* [254] about people whose lives and talents were attuned to the new business realities. These people were accused of wealth, and guilty of education. They shared common values, whether they were in Palo Alto or Madison, Wisconsin. The lifestyles of technology moguls began resembling those of Hollywood stars and producers. It became more obvious as the entertainment industry became dependent upon technology to make movies, and as video gaming became an industry.

Tech centers became magnets for talent from around the world, and tech lifestyles something to emulate. Every state had its Silicon Valley. I called the result "Techlandia."

## TECH SEIZES POWER

Just as I can date the turn from CDs to the Internet with precision, to late 1994, I can also tell you the day when technology began flexing its political muscle.

It was November 14, 2007. As part of what it called a series of "hangouts" with Presidential candidates, Google chairman Eric Schmidt sat across from a young Illinois Senator named Barack Obama, [255] to discuss issues of interest to technology. Obama was even given the answer to a tech question, concerning the handling of large databases.

---

254    You can buy the book here https://www.amazon.com/Rise-Creative-Class-Revisited-Revised-Expanded/dp/0465042481
255    The interview is still available at https://www.youtube.com/watch?v=m4yVlPqeZwo

"Well, a bubble sort would definitely not be the way to go," Obama said.

He passed the audition. The Obama campaign was driven by Google technology. It scaled the intimacy of volunteers with a huge database that could greet them personally, helping them meet specific neighbors with specific tasks, helping them register to vote. All the cloud computing and database management techniques Google had been working on for a decade would be found in the Obama tech campaign.

His opponents didn't know what hit them.

Google and other technology companies were richly rewarded for their help in 2008. Technologists were put in place running government agencies and programs. Expertise was suddenly sexy. Much of the 2009 stimulus was geared to technology, especially the HITECH stimulus, meant to make Electronic Health Records a standard.

It was all too easy. Despite the year's political drama, technology had relatively little trouble taking power in 2008. The economic recovery that began in 2009, and which continued for a decade, was also driven by technology companies. Companies that built the clouds, like Google, came to believe they could do no wrong. They were creating wealth beyond anyone's wildest schemes.

Technology seemed like a true meritocracy that could tell government to stay its hands from the market, but instead support it with things technology companies wanted, a virtuous cycle. These policies made urban homeowners rich and pushed those without high-level technology skills to the economic edge.

I saw this in 2011, when I took my family out for dim sum in an Atlanta suburb. Our inner-city home's value had risen nearly 10-fold since 1984, and we now had dozens of restaurants and chic shops within walking distance. But in Gwinnett County there were huge shopping centers without tenants, big box parking lots without cars in their parking lots, and a dying mall.

As a business reporter I have found there's a feel to economic despair. I can smell it, hear it, even taste it in the air. I felt it, smelled it, heard it, and tasted it that day.

The tech economy made winners of the Creative Class, and among those of who served Cloud Czars like Google and Amazon. But it made losers in the suburbs and exurbs left behind by the new economy. Middle managers became computer repair people. Real estate salesmen became Uber drivers. The gig economy's immense wealth was all held in stock values. It was all for the founders, their bankers, and their investors. Technology had created a new class structure and most Americans, after two hard economic crashes in less than a decade, no longer trusted it.

The seeds of a backlash had been sewn.

## Moore's Law of Health

The backlash would have been impossible without something I call Moore's Law of Health.

Moore's Law of Health means we live longer, healthier, more active lives than ever before, thanks to inventions made possible by the power of Moore's Law.

If you live to 65, my age in 2020, you're likely to live until age 83. At the 2019 Heidelberg Laureate Conference in Germany, I watched 89-year old Stephen Swale explain the mathematics of a heartbeat, straight from memory, using just a blackboard. That would have been highly unlikely a century before, even a generation before. But we took it for granted. Men who invented the Internet's key technologies in the 1970s, like Vint Cerf [256](TCP/IP) and Martin Hellman [257] (private key cryptography), were still politically and physically active in 2021.

This is a wonderful thing. If like me you're over 65 and still active, you probably agree.

But our views of the world around us seldom change much as we age. The assumptions we create in our 20s usually follow us throughout our lives. People who fought the Vietnam War will fight it until their

256 Here is Vint Cerf's Wikipedia entry. https://en.wikipedia.org/wiki/Vint_Cerf
257 Martin Hellman's Wikipedia entry https://en.wikipedia.org/wiki/Martin_Hellman

dying day, just as their great grandfathers "waved the bloody shirt" of the Civil War, thinking of Democrats as traitors, for the rest of their lives.

The result is political lag. Just as Moore's Law is accelerating change, Moore's Law of Health threatens to put it into reverse. The Vietnam War was a living, breathing issue in the 2016 campaign, even though it had been over for 40 years. The median age of that year's voters was higher than it had ever been. Their economic assumptions were formed in the era of oil, not the era of technology.

We're paying a very high price for Moore's Law of Health. Trump and Trumpism are the price. A President and government dedicated to fighting what's growing, and protecting what's not, is the price of Moore's Law of Health.

## Extremism in the Age of Technology

Newton's Third Law of Motion states that "for every action there is an equal and opposite reaction."

This is true in politics as in everything else. For every political action, there is an equal and opposite reaction.

Whenever a new industry rises to power, an older industry must lose power. The old industry clings to power for as long as it can, but inevitably there is a crisis. Only one side can win. The new leaders displace the old.

That's what the Civil War was, railroads rising and agriculture falling. That's what the Progressive Era meant, railroads falling and utilities rising. That's what the Great Depression meant, manufacturers rising and utilities falling. That's what the 1970s meant, the fall of manufacturing and the rise of oil.

In 2009 tech first replaced oil at the center of the economy. The values of the technology industry, its need for human capital trumping that of land and resources, grated on the people left behind by the change.

Barack Obama symbolized technology's new myths, its values, and its power. He didn't look like any President before him, yet he had an elite education. He was comfortable with the new world of technology and celebrity. He could use the Internet, it seemed, as adroitly as previous leaders used TV, the way Franklin Roosevelt used radio and the movies, the way Theodore Roosevelt used magazines, the way Abraham Lincoln's speeches moved millions when printed in newspapers.

The Tea Party backlash was organized by resource billionaires, oilmen and manufacturers whose relative wealth was being drained by the rise of the Cloud Czars -- Google, Microsoft, Apple, Amazon.Com and Facebook.

By 2021 the Czars they were worth $7 trillion taken together. In corporate terms all remain youngsters. Facebook hadn't even been founded until 2004. But its market cap was four times that of AT&T, whose role it supplanted, especially in the developing world.

The political backlash crafted by resource billionaires like Charles and David Koch was joined by all the new economy's losers -- farmers, middle managers, salesmen, repairmen, truck drivers, all the TV-watching hordes whose lives were being turned upside down by the rise of the Internet.

It was natural that a TV star, Donald Trump, would become the movement's spokesman. TV had been the resource era's dominant medium. Trump and his movement were able to hack the Internet through social media, at a fraction of what Google had paid the Obama campaign. Trump amassed millions of Twitter and Facebook followers, and the propaganda rolled right into the followers' heads, unfiltered.

Because the public Internet had scaled, unregulated social discourse was now an industry. Because a subculture of hackers had risen to feed off the Internet's wealth, Trump was able to work alongside other oil producers, in Russia and Saudi Arabia, with promises to Make America Great Again and achieve power.

The shock of 2016 was still reverberating in the technology industry as I began to revise this book in 2019. I have compared it in my journalism to how oilmen seethed watching Jimmy Carter attack them in his cardigan sweater.[258] I have compared it to how the Great Depression's deflation shocked manufacturers into a new political alignment, and how the Progressive Era caused capital to create regulated utilities.

Technology was coddled by policymakers for a generation and won power in 2008 almost without opposition. In 2019 its position is being seriously threatened by an older, obsolete business model.

As I reviewed the last paragraphs in 2021, it was remarkable how prescient they seemed. The Internet industry did indeed regain power in 2020, albeit narrowly. The intensity of the rage Trump generated energized the entire Democratic Party. It turned a moderate Vice President, Joe Biden, into a Reagan-like figure, quietly leading a revolution focused on tech's needs to create, and maintain, human capital.

The lesson of 2020 seems clear. People are infrastructure, too. This will reverberate in American politics for decades.

## THE MOORE CRISIS

Economic growth always has a gating factor, something that limits how fast an economy can grow.

For manufacturers it was demand for finished products. For oil it was the cost of developing new fields, including overcoming political opposition to that development.

For technology, the gating factor to growth is the cost of human capital. Tech needs talent. It needs highly motivated brains of all types.

A single mind, given the right training, the right incentives, and the freedom to let their imagination go where it will, can create 1,000 times the value of any ordinary worker. Given the right incentives and tools, they can disrupt any industry or business model.

Some people call data the new oil, but it's in refineries that oil

<hr>

258     I called Trump a "Bizarro Carter" after the 2016 election. https://www.danablankenhorn.com/2016/11/bizarro-carter.html Trump is Carter's opposite in every way, and just as out of touch with tech as Carter was with oil a generation ago.

becomes fuel and plastic. Anyone can have a child, but it's universities that are the refineries of our time. It takes a trained mind to refine data, with software, into a new, more efficient economic order. Great minds are the Hope Diamonds of our world.

The more of these minds your society has, the more unconstrained their imaginations, the more they can learn, the more capital becomes available to them, the more your society will grow in the 21st century. Restricting minds in any way inhibits growth.

There are many ways to limit human capital. You can imprison minds behind ideologies, behind religions, or behind a vast network of surveillance technology. You can limit human mobility and slow technology's growth rate. You can encourage ignorance.

The biggest ideological enemy of technology is ultra-nationalism. The problems of the 21$^{st}$ century are global in scale and scope. The COVID-19 pandemic can't end until nations act in concert. Climate change can't be addressed by any single nation, just as infrastructure can't be built on behalf of any single company. Nationalist ideologies that created demand for the guns of World War II are pollution in a technological age. Tariff wars are unhealthy for economies and other living things. Wars for territory are useless. People can move.

Technological progress is also necessary if there is to be a 22nd century. Without solutions to the problems created by railroads, utilities, manufacturers and oil, Earth will throw off mankind the same way it throws off any virus. It will simply run a fever until the virus, that is us, is destroyed.

The technologies created by Moore's Law, then, are also the gating factor to the continuing existence of the human species.

## TECH'S CHIEF ENEMY

Tech's chief political enemy is technology itself.

It comes down to an old saying I've loaded onto my own Twitter page. "If you don't take responsibility for the medium you create then someone else will. And they won't have your interests at heart." [259]

I first became involved with online etiquette, or "netiquette," in the late 1980s. Early adopters of online discussion technology, like the Meta Network, [260] were highly educated professionals, deeply concerned with ethical issues. But it was obvious even then that other people were not. Even in 1988 I found online political discussions devolving into something like Monty Python's Argument Clinic[261] sketch, with people disagreeing just to be disagreeable.

Early online forums charged users for each hour of use, and this money helped fund moderators who kept things level. Once the Internet made access free, this funding was lost, and moderators disappeared. Content itself became free as Web sites evolved into social networks. Human moderation didn't scale, so it simply wasn't provided. This let companies like Google and Facebook bring one-third of their revenue to the net income line.

Trump was the best-known politician to hack this system, to build online mobs who would defend lies as truth. But it's easy to do. It costs no money. In 2021 Trump acolytes dominate the most-viewed lists on Facebook [262]. Their interests are not Facebook's interest. Their interests are their own.

Their success is based on a natural algorithm most web sites use that many believe is now killing democracy and threatening the social networks.

you look at a lot of stories about the Atlanta Braves, news algorithms will give you more stories about the Atlanta Braves. If you constantly check out bird feeders at Amazon, you'll see more bird feeders.

At the same time if you like a collection of violent videos, you'll

---

259 It's called a "pinned tweet." https://twitter.com/danablankenhorn
260 Learn more about the Meta Network on Wikipedia. https://en.wikipedia.org/wiki/The_Meta_Network
261 Here it is performed, from YouTube. https://www.youtube.com/watch?v=DkQhK8O9Jik
262 This list is from July 2020 https://www.socialmediatoday.com/news/facebook-shares-new-insights-into-most-shared-posts-on-its-platform/582138/

get more violent videos. If you are intrigued by political agitation, you will see more of that. People are easily sucked down "rabbit holes" like this, and there's a huge industry of people, often funded by politicians, to lead them along. The costs are as low as typing or pointing a camera at yourself. Distribution costs nothing.

Rules should be set, but who will set them? If the answer is government those rules will favor the government. If those rules are the network owner, those rules will favor the network. Facebook's effort to create its own Oversight Board [263] was highly controversial, especially after it upheld the suspension of Trump's account.

Twitter has had more success. It has spent more money on human moderators, compared with total revenue, and thus its profit margins are lower than Facebook's. Its aim is to tone down rhetoric, to cool tempers, and to keep malicious actors from spreading malice.

But it's the underlying algorithms that are the problem. Congress is threatening to repeal Section 230, which holds networks harmless from what their users do. [264]But that would force networks to err on the side of caution, driving all political discussion underground.

Ultimately, tech's power over society means tech has responsibility for society. You can't maintain one without accepting the other.

## ONE MORE THING...

There is one more thing that technology can do if it's thwarted.

It can move.

Technology is fungible. It will grow wherever it is given room to grow. Moore's Law, PCs and the Internet may have been American

263 The making of the Facebook tribunal was described in *The New Yorker* https://www.newyorker.com/tech/annals-of-technology/inside-the-making-of-facebooks-supreme-court
264 A 2021 Congressional hearing was covered by CNBC https://www.cnbc.com/2021/04/27/facebook-youtube-twitter-execs-testify-in-senate-on-algorithms.html Both political parties want the others' speech limited and their own unlimited.

creations, but the next technology doesn't have to be.

If we won't import people from India, India will define the next generation of technology. It's already doing a lot of that. Israel has so many start-ups, drawing so much capital from U.S. companies, that it could easily attain the scale to keep the next generation of progress to itself.

Most semiconductors are already made in China. Just because a government hands out freedom with an eye dropper, doesn't mean technology can't be created there if its supply of human capital here is limited. Companies like Alibaba, TenCent Holdings, Pinduoduo, JD.Com, Bytedance, and Baidu. They're achieving greater scale within their market than the American Cloud Czars have in their home market. That's why China's leaders acted against them starting late in 2020, creating an antitrust regime. Meanwhile many stores and cities in China are more advanced than ours because privacy activists can't object to the changes. Chinese entrepreneurs will be happy to beat us to the next big thing.

Only one thing is certain with Moore's Law. There will be a next big thing. Cloud computing won't remain the sole province of five Cloud Czars. Organizations of all sizes can buy systems working on similar principles today and use open source technology to adapt to them. Competition is fierce at the bleeding edge. There are no guarantees.

America is not guaranteed in the world of Moore's Law. We may have started out this century ahead. It doesn't mean we'll finish there. To stay there both our economic and political systems must adapt to the demands of Moore's Law. That means we need a flexible economy, where people and companies are free to fail as well as succeed. It also means we need a flexible polity, in which elections are honest and the people can change their minds. The result should be a flexible society, where people are allowed the greatest possible amount of ordered liberty.

America's Constitutional principles are perfectly in sync with the demands of Moore's Law. The only question is whether they will be retained.

# Chapter 11
# Moore's Law of Content

As I discussed in the previous chapter, Moore's Law has corollaries that present real challenges.

- **Moore's Second Law** means the cost of building chip plants keeps rising with their complexity. It means that over time there are fewer companies making chips.

- **Moore's Law of Health** creates **Moore's Law of Politic**s, so society is led by people whose assumptions are tied to the distant past.

To that we need to add **Moore's Law of Content**, which offsets **Moore's Law of Software**.

## Moore's Law of Content

### Software runs. Content is Absorbed.

Content, of all types, is different from software. Software keeps adding value each time it runs. If your software processes credit card transactions for a penny, it keeps earning that penny each time it runs.

Content doesn't work that way. Once you absorb content it's absorbed. You might absorb the content multiple times, but there's a limit.

Take this book for example. Once you read it, you've read it. You may read it a second time. You may even refer to it later. But its economic value to you is exhausted once you put it on the shelf.

If you really like this book, you may give it to a friend. A library lets the same book be read several times. But the creator of the book gets no additional value from that loan. Software, by contrast, keeps providing value every time it's used. It can't be lent, and it's generally not even owned. Instead, it's licensed, and whether it's from an update or a yearly subscription, it keeps collecting economic value for its maker as it ages.

Moore's Law of Content applies to all kinds of content, although creators of video content had yet to fully comprehend this as this book was being written. They think this is the start of their golden age.

It's not. Anyone familiar with Moore's Law can look at video's future by looking at the recent past of print content and music.

## MOORE IN PRINT

If this were a hardback book, bought at retail, you would have paid $20 for it. (I wish)

Most of that $20 would go to marketing. An author is lucky to get 30%. My early books gave me commissions of just 15%. Some writers, whose names are so well-known their books sell themselves, do a bit better.

Figure $6 per book. If the publisher sells out a typical mid-market print run of 10,000 books, that's $60,000 in my pocket. From that, my cost of producing the book, the time I spent slaving over it, must be taken out, and it usually is in the form of an advance against royalties. Writers want as big an advance as possible, not just so they can eat while writing, but because a bigger advance means the publisher will work hard for their book, having already invested in it.

A best-seller with 100,000 copies, written by someone like Stephen King whose name goes above the title, is profitable for everyone. Since the author keeps their book copyright, King can re-sell the book's paperback rights, then sell the video rights. Stephen King's name assures that those rights will mean big bucks with no extra work.

The point is that Stephen King earns a good living. But most writers aren't Stephen King.

The cost of printing and marketing a book assures that its retail price will be firm. Even if the author is, say, Dana Blankenhorn, that $20 retail price on the hardback is fixed. Until, that is, the book stops selling. Then the price starts dropping. As time goes by, after people finish their copies, the book goes into a second-hand shop at just a few dollars, and I get none of that money.

Writing books, then, is dicey in the best of times. But what happens when that book goes online?

A file containing the complete text of this book is just 100 kilobytes. Downloading it in 2019 takes just a few seconds. Just as with software, its distribution cost is zero. But its utility isn't unlimited, the way software's utility is unlimited. To gain economic value it must find new readers. The value of an online book drops as it's distributed, while the value of software increases as more people use it.

## The Platform

Readers and writers have had over a decade now to adapt to Moore's Law of Content.

"Superstores" for books have disappeared. Borders went bust. Barnes & Noble is heading there. Smaller bookstores have survived, helped by their small size and low-cost structures. Some have survived by focusing on specific niches, like kids. Others have done it by focusing on local readers, with special events and book-signings.

The market's primary adaptation has been the Amazon Kindle.

The Kindle isn't just an e-book reader. It's not even just a bookstore. The 2010 version of this book was published on the Kindle, and only later offered in print. That may be the case with this version.

Over the last decade it has become increasingly easy to produce both a Kindle book and an accompanying print edition. Kindle takes Word documents. Kindle helps writers choose cover art. Kindle can even run spelling and grammar checks before accepting a manuscript, so writers don't maik mistakes they don't mean to make.

Amazon is also something new in the book world. It's a platform. It seeks the maximum return from every type of reader, and can even deliver a living to self-published writers, whose royalties can reach 70% of their books' cover price.

They do this in a variety of ways.

First, like every other part of the Amazon store, they watch what their customers are buying and offer them follow-on purchases of interest. If you buy a hardback at the Amazon store you may soon find yourself facing ads for the same book or closely related books on other Web sites.

If you buy a book's Kindle version, you'll pay less than you will for the hardback. The price is determined by the author and/or publisher. The price of best-sellers is driven by publishers, but few are more than $15. Many are under $10.

There are also a host of Kindle books costing anywhere from 99 cents to $5. Unlike the remainders you'll find at a used bookstore, these are often first-editions, self-published. The royalty may be 35%, or it may be 70%. Marketing is all up to the author. They can buy ads on Amazon.Com just as other resellers do. When you publish a Kindle book, you'll be asked to categorize it, by fiction genres or non-fiction subjects. This will drive Amazon's search engine and can also drive the writer-publisher's advertising.

Then there is Kindle Unlimited. This is a streaming service for books. For $10 per month, you can read as many books as you want from the Kindle Unlimited library.

Authors have found a variety of ways to get the most from the platform. Many fiction writers create series, with the same main characters or setting, that readers will devour the way they might binge-watch a TV show on Netflix. Others put the first book of a series on

Kindle Unlimited, then charge for the following books. Is $5/book the best price? Is $10? Writers experiment on pricing, they communicate with one another on Amazon forums, and they gain insights directly from Amazon, which wants to sell a lot of books.

Writers who learn how to market through the platform can make a decent living. It can be better than what they would have gotten from a publisher, because their costs are low, and royalties can be high.

Readers get a great deal. They can soak up any genre they want, going down a "rabbit hole" of suggestions with similar plots the way a Facebook user or YouTube viewer is accustomed to their favorite content.

Amazon gets the best deal. They get subscription revenue from Kindle Unlimited, they get a fat percentage from every book and, because it's mostly a digital business, their costs are small.

The power of owning a platform is going to be increasingly important as Moore's Law of Content moves into music and video.

## Moore News (or Less)

Moore's Law of Content really bites in the business I grew up in, which is journalism.

When the Web was first spun, 25 years ago, journalism had a "free" business model. That is, the price you paid for a newspaper or a magazine didn't go to the writers and editors. It went to the cost of getting that paper to you, it went into distribution.

Only 8% of a newspaper's budget went to editorial. There was a news budget only because of advertising. A generation ago a newspaper ad salesman could tell a car dealer, based on surveys, that 10,000 of his newspaper's readers would pass that dealership every day, and that an ad in the paper would generate 10 sales over the course of a month. A bigger ad would generate more sales. The same was true for local department stores. The big circulation of a big-city newspaper even made small text ads, for help wanted or garage sales or people looking for love, valuable profit centers.

The Internet destroyed this business model.

The newspaper's database was built only on their subscribers. Publishers could offer rough demographics on subscribers, and magazines were narrowly targeted to industries and lifestyles, making their data more valuable. But in the end, this was an intrinsic business model. The newspaper or magazine was aggregating readers based on a shared location, industry, or lifestyle, THEN selling access to these people through ads.

The Internet let companies like Google track all users through invisible "cookies" loaded onto Web pages in the background, collected by browsers, then analyzed as large databases in clouds. They took advantage of Moore's Law of Software, and the rest of Moore's Laws, so that advertisers could reach the tiniest groups, for the same cost as if they bought the whole network.

Recent "innovations by Google[265] and Apple [266], aimed at making their technology less intrusive to user privacy, don't change the basic equation. They're selling ads extrinsically, based on who is accessing the content, rather than intrinsically, based on interests generated by the content itself.

For just a few dollars, car dealers using this new extrinsic business model could buy likely prospects for the same price as undifferentiated prospects. Google captured the segmentation value of the audience, sharing the savings with the advertisers. Advertisers could use these savings to deliver many more ad impressions to chosen prospects. Newspaper ads dried up.

Instead of getting 8% of a big pie, newspaper editorial was now getting no pie. No pie to print the newspaper, no pie to sell ads in it, no

265    Google calls its technology Federated Learning of Cohorts (FLoC). https://blog.google/products/ads-commerce/2021-01-privacy-sandbox/

266    Apple calls its new technology the App Tracking Transparency (ATT) framework. https://developer.apple.com/documentation/apptrackingtransparency Apps won't be allowed to collect personal information by default, but will still be able to sell ads based on demographics.

pie for anyone.

Then Moore's Law of Content really took hold. Once news is absorbed, it's absorbed. You only need to read the headlines once, and then their utility is gone. You only need to hear a story once, and its economic value is lost to you.

Moore's Law of Content made printing news from a wire service useless. Only exclusives had economic value, and this was extremely time-limited as the essence of those exclusives was shared among readers.

With the ad-based business model gone, publishers are left with stark choices. They could charge readers for access to their news, putting up paywalls, but that dramatically limited their audience. Their stories will leak out as people start talking about them, and the whole point of news is to get people talking about it.

Most eventually decided that this choice was no choice at all. The news that comes "free" online today mostly comes from TV networks (subsidized by other network fees) or politically-biased sites (subsidized by politicians). This is a serious threat to democracy. If the only news the average citizen can get online comes with political strings attached, will they be able to find an objective truth on which to base their votes?

This is also happening in the finance beat I've been over the last decade. For the last two years I've been writing at *InvestorPlace*, a financial opinion site. They sell access to my stories to sites like Yahoo Finance. Other sites, dubbed "scrapers" in the trade, also repost them without permission. *InvestorPlace* gets some ad revenue when people see my stories on the main site, they get more from their traffic at Yahoo, but they get nothing from the scrapers. All these sites compete with one another to sell "memberships," offering data on stocks for analysis alongside their stories, but the market for this up-sell is limited. Increasingly, even this limited financial analysis is going behind paywalls, at sites like *Marketwatch, Business Insider* and *Seeking Alpha*.

I'm lucky. Most technology journalists aren't doing nearly as well. Many are now reduced to writing for vendors or doing other forms of public relations. Others have retired early

The same thing is happening on other beats.

In sports, sites like *The Players' Forum"* have cut out the middleman, with stories that are "written" (or ghost-written) by athletes themselves. These are people who used to be sources, but they now give reporters no comment and make money as publishers.

In politics, patronage has replaced advertising as a business model. Stories become propaganda, much as they were in the 1790s, when Federalists and Democratic-Republicans paid printers and writers directly to condemn Thomas Jefferson or Alexander Hamilton.

The Medill School of Journalism, from which I got a M.S. in journalism (with an emphasis on magazines) in 1978, now describes itself as a journalism "and integrated marketing" program. (I feel like burning my degree.)

## Moore Music

The impact of Moore's Law of Content first became apparent in the music business 20 years ago, with the rise of Napster.

Napster, and its imitators, let people copy music files from CDs and share them online. CDs, like books, had a functioning business model. You'd pay $15-20 for a disk, you would listen to it as much as you wanted, and the artists got a royalty for each disk sold.

But Napster offered no royalty. It was the equivalent of making Stephen King's latest best-seller free to everyone. People no longer bought CDs. The business model disappeared.

Music does carry some of the values of software. You will listen to a song you like many times. Having lots of people memorize a song means the artist who made it can get cash from concerts. But a concert tour is hard work. It's just as hard as writing and producing the song in the first place. And not all artists like touring. The Beatles stopped touring within a few years of coming to America and spent most of their career in the studio. What if Napster had existed in the 1960s?

The Internet shifted the music industry's business model, away from albums, collections of 10-12 songs that could generate $15 from a buyer, toward single tracks. Artists were forced into a treadmill, driven by Moore's Law of Software, to write only hits.

To stop the "piracy" of systems like Napster, companies like Spotify created a new model of "streaming." For a fixed monthly charge, customers can listen to as many songs as we want. It's really a legal version of Napster, with a bigger library.

But this is even worse for artists.

Think about a song. Do you know its name, and the artist? If you don't, it's going to be hard to call it up on a service like Amazon Music.

Unless the song's publisher has already put a big effort behind making a song a hit, you're not going to ask for it. You might ask for the artist. You might then be offered music from similar artists. This can help you find new music. But the utility of any song, or collection of songs, goes down.

The streaming services pay artists a pittance for each hearing anyway.

Even well-respected musical artists now get monthly checks that are barely worth cashing.


## Moore Video

Moore's Law of Content is only just now working against the video business, but to those who understand it the future has already been written.

There are already hints of what's coming. Here's what I wrote in 2010:

I haven't set foot in a movie theater in a year. Neither have most people. Movies are like hardback books. They cost $10 and more per ticket, for a single view.

Because grownups don't go to the movies the only movies that matter today are "Spandex" movies, the equivalent of cartoons. Their effects benefit from Moore's Law, becoming more spectacular each year, but the technology is the star. Actors play one-dimensional parts in front of green screens.

Movies are still made because of "ancillary" rights. Movies are exported to a global market, so today China is more important to studios than the U.S. They go from theaters to "pay per view," which used to be the DVD window. Then they're sold for broadcast. Then to cable networks. If the movie does well it can be resold for years or even decades, something that wasn't possible when Hollywood was at its height in the 1940s.

TV shows also have had ancillary income. After they run on the network that produced them, they might be sold in syndication to other TV stations, for "stripping" five days a week. This has made late 20th century TV stars like Jerry Seinfeld wealthy. Stardom let actors do TV commercials or go to Broadway. The "residuals" from rebroadcast mean even many retired actors are doing well. Stardom also has economic value by itself.

While production costs have caused many TV networks to create cheap "reality" shows or game shows with little syndication value, cable still offers positive economics for the operators. To assure we have something to watch, cable households pay $150 per month, or more, for a menu of hundreds of channels, on which there may be several watchable shows on at any one time. Old movies, and old TV shows, still have syndication value. News channels get a set fee per subscriber each month, and so do sport channels.

Just as TV networks have responded to rising costs by going to reality TV, so news and sports channels have responded to rising costs by going to talk. Most of what they offer today are people sitting in a studio, expressing outrage over what's happening. The sport channels still cover games, but TV news "bureaus" have disappeared. You no longer see what happens. You watch people talk about it.

A decade later, everything is about streaming.

If you have Netflix, or Amazon Prime, you don't need cable. Instead of having a few dozen shows to choose from, you have hundreds, even thousands. You can watch just what you want to watch. You're no longer beholden to a broadcast or cable schedule. There are no day parts. There's no more waiting for the next episode -- you can binge a whole season in a day. Cord-cutting is growing. There's less money for cable networks. Some are even going out of business.

Life has changed for producers as well.

Netflix pays the full costs of production, but there may be no ancillary rights. If TV or cable audiences dry up, where else can something be sold? Netflix is a global platform, so the money from opening in separate markets, or selling shows to separate markets, is also gone. You set your budget, you pay your people, you hope enough people watch so you'll get another season, or another deal. But the platform, not the producer, is now in charge.

Now here's what no one understands, especially as we enter the 2020s.

The gating factor to entertainment is no longer how much are you willing to pay for a cable subscription. It's how many streaming services can you watch? A day is 24 hours for everyone, regardless of income.

Take my current life as just one example.

I get Amazon Prime "free." I buy free shipping and all the streaming comes at no added cost. I could pay $10/month without free shipping, but that's still a bargain. So is Netflix, at $13/month.

Walt Disney was desperate to get into this business in 2019, desperate enough to take some big losses. In 2019 they charged just $5/month for "ESPN+," which shows hundreds of games at once. Not people talking about games, but real games. At the same time Disney was getting $9/

month per subscriber for ESPN. If I kept my cable subscription, ESPN was doing all right. But once that's gone, so is their cash flow.

The same is true for "Disney+," their new streaming service, said to be the industry's greatest success story in 2021 with 100 million subscribers. To reach that number Disney bundled both ESPN+ and Disney+ with Hulu, an existing streaming service, at $13/month That's the same price as Netflix' most popular package. The assumption is that, once they grab an audience, Disney can start raising that price.

Can they? With AT&T, Comcast and CBS/Viacom also offering streaming products, not to mention cable programmers like Discovery, how many services does anyone really need? Remember, instead of choosing from among the shows that are "on" now, streaming lets you choose anything, at any time, from libraries with thousands of shows.

Then consider other cable channels. As more people cut the cable cord what happens to CNN and MSNBC? Can the news channels really charge $10 per month for talking heads? How big will their audiences be? How many will buy libraries of documentaries, along with their Netflix and Hulu and Amazon Prime?

There's a limit to the video market, based on Moore's Law of Content.

That limit is time.

I only have a few hours each day for TV. I work. So do most people. I know that many bars and restaurants keep a TV on all day and night, but that's only one channel. Maybe, in the case of a sports bar, they'll pay for a full line-up of content, but only sports content.

The same thing that happened in print, the same thing that happened in music, is about to happen in video. We pay less, we get more, thanks to Moore's Law of Software. But content creators don't get more. They get less.

How will writers, musicians and (soon) TV and movie producers react to what Moore's Law of Content has in store for them?

Stay tuned.

# CHAPTER 12

# MOORE'S FAULT

Moore's Law means technology gets better and better faster and faster.

But it has corollaries and byproducts we must deal with.

- **Moore's Law** itself is offset by **Moore's Second Law**, because the cost of setting up chip production, including environmental costs, goes up with complexity.

- **Moore's Law of Health** is offset by **Moore's Law of Politics**, which means political change is increasingly stuck in the past as we hurtle into the future.

- **Moore's Law of Software** is offset by **Moore's Law of Content**, because the utility of books, music or movies decreases once you've experienced it.

To that we should add the concept of Technology Debt, the need to constantly replace infrastructure as it becomes obsolete. This lets new businesses develop, while tearing entire industries down.

In 2019 and 2020 all the negative aspects of Moore's Law seemed to come crashing down at once, threatening the world created by Moore's Law.

Government control over the economy slowed the pace of change just as we need to accelerate it, increasing technology debt. Even government oversight can slow Moore's Law, as in the case of Microsoft, because companies will adapt by hiring lawyers, lobbyists and bureaucrats who all say no to change.

Despite the risks, it's necessary that we accelerate change if we're to survive this century.

The environmental destruction created by the Industrial Revolution, its reliance on fossil fuels, its scaled farming and ranching, has accelerated in the 21st century. When I came back to this book in 2019, it was clear that it was no longer even possible to save the globe's ice caps, or prevent a catastrophe threatening all life on the planet, by conventional means.

We're going to have to invent our way out of this. We're going to have to double down on the products of Moore's Law.

Even absent political will we saw, in the 2010s, some hopeful signs. Solar panels and windmills now produce electricity for less than coal, and for less than gas, when infrastructure costs are included. New materials like graphene, made from carbon, can replace lithium for batteries. Tesla has proven there is a market for electric cars. In 2019 you could buy Impossible Burgers or Beyond Burgers that don't contain meat.

The pace of scientific discovery keeps increasing as a direct result of Moore's Law. I could call this Moore's Law of Science, but not in this edition.

Moore's Law made all this possible. The ability to connect people and ideas, the ability to run mathematical models in an instant, accelerates change in every direction. This includes negative as well as positive change. Put Moore's Law in the hands of terrorists or autocrats, and the implications become obvious.

In this chapter I'm going to examine some of the negative implications of Moore's Law, not in the hope of stopping change, but in directing it in useful directions, limiting the impact of its byproducts.

I'll start with some things that are not bugs in the law but features of it.

## MOORE DEFLATION

Moore's Law creates deflation.

Deflation is, as we saw during the Great Depression, even worse than the inflation that plagued the economy in the 1970s, the early years of oil's dominance. When prices rise quickly your paycheck is worth less. When prices fall, you lose your paycheck.

The solution to this offered by the Obama Administration was to offset deflation by printing more money. It worked, for a while. Money poured back into banks let them lend. Money borrowed for the stimulus created more spending.

But Moore's Law is relentless and accelerating. Simply printing money isn't a solution. Money left in a vault, or in a stock's market cap, isn't doing anything. In this way money is a verb, not a noun. It only has an impact when it's being used.

What money was used for in the 2010s was to accelerate Moore's Law's economic impact, turning software loose on markets and long-held economic relationships. Companies like Uber and Lyft replaced both the jobs of taxi drivers and their regulators. Facebook, Twitter, and Google News replaced both the news business and those societal systems meant to separate truth from lies.

The money earned by all this also went directly into asset values. The five Cloud Czars -- Microsoft, Apple, Amazon, Google, and Facebook -- came to be worth over $4.5 trillion. The companies supplying them with hardware and software like Intel, Nvidia and Cisco Systems, and the companies using their clouds to create new services, like Netflix and Salesforce.Com, came to be worth trillions more.

This means asset values in 2019 are vulnerable to a panic. Microsoft's market cap is over $1 trillion because the last trade, if applied against all shares, totals over $1 trillion. If shares trade lower, the market cap can drop, and there's no real bottom. The same is true for home prices.

Moore's Law in 2019 continues to build incredible wealth, but it places that wealth in fewer-and-fewer hands.

# Bill Gates Loses at Brewster's Billions

No one illustrates this better than Bill Gates.

Gates made his fortune from Moore's Law of Software, mostly in the era where software was "shrink-wrapped," sold in boxes under restrictive software licenses. Gates was able to control this market by controlling the operating system under which applications worked, first under license from IBM, then on his own through Microsoft Windows. This was seen as a monopoly by the government, and Microsoft was unable to capitalize on the Internet era as it hoped to when it launched news sites like MSNBC.

Gates "retired" from Microsoft in 2008 to devote himself full-time to philanthropy. He promised that his Bill and Melinda Gates Foundation[267] would give away most of his Microsoft fortune. Berkshire Hathaway CEO Warren Buffett also signed a Giving Pledge[268] and added his own fortune to Gates' endeavor. (In 2021 the Gates announced they were divorcing, and as this was written the eventual size of the Foundation was in doubt.)

Since its launch, the Gates Foundation has built an enormous bureaucracy in Seattle, dedicated to giving away this money in a responsible way.[269] There are nearly 1,500 employees. Through the end of 2018 they had made grants totaling $50 billion. The value of its endowment was estimated at $46.8 billion.

The Gates don't want to be a government. They want to make sure the causes they support are right, that money isn't wasted, and that there are benchmarks for success. But the effect of creating a bureaucracy in the name of deciding where money should go, and measuring its effectiveness, created its own form of government, a private one.

Meanwhile, Gates and Buffett keep building their fortunes.

---

267 Here is the Gates Foundation home page. https://www.gatesfoundation.org/
268 The giving pledge was covered by CNBC https://www.cnbc.com/2018/02/13/why-bill-and-melinda-gates-give-away-billions.html
269 Here is the Foundation's fact sheet on that. https://www.gatesfoundation.org/who-we-are/general-information/foundation-factsheet

In 2018, Bill Gates gave away $35 billion but, by keeping most of his money in stock, the value of his fortune increased by $16 billion.[270] As a result, Gates has come to support higher estate taxes and even dropped his opposition to a wealth tax. In 1921 his fortune was estimated at $130 billion by Forbes. [271] His divorce seems to be the only event that could cause him to die wealthier than he is now.

It's like the movie *Brewster's Millions*, first made in 1945 and remade 40 years later, the remake starring Richard Pryor and John Candy. [272] Brewster is given a large amount of money and told that if he can spend it by a deadline, he'll get a fortune. In the movie Brewster gets in under the deadline. Gates' pile is rising faster than he can spend it.

Gates isn't the only software gazillionaire being made ultra-wealthy by stock. As this was written 5 of the world's 10 centi-billionaires were American tech tycoons – Gates, Elon Musk, Mark Zuckerberg, Larry Ellison, and Larry Page. (Page's partner at Google, Sergey Brin, was right behind him.) How they deal with their enormous fortunes could determine whether Americans continue supporting the political and economic systems which made them. [273]

## MOORE UNEMPLOYMENT

There is another byproduct of deflation caused by Moore's Law, which is unemployment. Like deflation, this is a feature of Moore's Law, not a bug, although it's often seen as one by critics and those who are victims of it.

Moore's Law has created deflation, concentrated wealth in the form of stock, and unemployed millions of educated people. The

270 https://fortune.com/2019/09/17/bill-gates-net-worth-2019-money-strategy-investing-taxes/

271 Forbes keeps a real-time estimate of billionaire wealth in front of its firewall. https://www.forbes.com/real-time-billionaires/#73cbd7b73d78

272 There is an even earlier production, from 1921, starring Fatty Arbuckle. https://www.imdb.com/title/tt0011998/

273 I have been covering this issue at my personal blog. https://www.danablankenhorn.com/2021/05/techs-stock-problem.html

unemployment of educated people has caused a backlash against technology. I've sometimes dismissed these critics as Luddites,[274] like the men and women who took to destroying looms in England early in the industrial age, as machines replaced handmade cloth.

But these are people. They need answers. If the beneficiaries of Moore's Law won't deliver those answers, they'll go elsewhere. They'll go to Trump, even though his policies punish high-value technology in favor of lower-value oil and manufacturing.

In the 20th century, Moore's Law productivity meant more work was being done for less money. In the 21st century, Moore's Law replaced whole layers of middle managers in the 2000s. It replaced large numbers of market makers in the 2010s -- bankers, brokers, and traders. These were considered highly skilled jobs. Many carried big salaries. Once they're done by software, they don't come back.

In the wake of the COVID pandemic this created what was called a "k-shaped" recovery. Wealthy people, and those with tech jobs they could do from home, recovered very quickly. Meanwhile, restaurant and hotel workers lost their jobs. Enormous piles of cash went to investors, who put that cash "to work" in the form of assets, from stocks and bonds to Bitcoin and houses, that quickly rose in value. Inequality became a chasm, thanks to Moore's Law.

In the wake of this, what are the victims of Moore's Law supposed to think? What are they supposed to do?

## MOORE'S LAW OF MARKETS

Inequality is made worse by the nature of technology markets in the era of Moore's Law.

Moore's Law of Markets is that the winner takes the pot.

It has become a tradition in the technology business that whichever

---

274    The Wikipedia page on the Luddite movement https://en.wikipedia.org/wiki/Luddite

company dominates a niche wins 90% of it, and nearly all its profits. A second competitor may get 9% of the market and run at close to break-even. Everyone else gets the other 1% of the market and eventually gives up.

In the 1990s it created what was called the "WinTel" monopoly. Intel chips, and Microsoft software, controlled 90% of the old PC market. The companies that sought to compete with it, AMD in chips and Apple in operating systems, got just 9% of it, and were only marginally profitable. Everyone else fought for scraps and lost money doing it.

This hasn't changed in the 21st century. All five of the companies that invested most heavily in the cloud were being accused of monopoly power in 2019. This was true for Amazon in e-commerce, of Facebook in social networking, of Google in search, of Apple and Microsoft in their markets.

The problem goes beyond the Cloud Czars. Once a market becomes established, it quickly becomes the "property" of one company. The need of a market to scale, and the advantage this gives to incumbents, continues to give what look like monopoly profits to a very small number of corporate founders and the people backing them.

The way America has funded, and rewarded, growth for over a century now is the stock market. New wealth is reflected primarily in the price of stock.

Asked in the early 1980s for stock tips, former Federal Reserve chair Paul Volcker is said to have answered, "prices will fluctuate." Today they mainly fluctuate up, as assets are piled on assets.

In the 1970s, technology helped to spread wealth around through the rise of mutual funds and the beginning of discount brokerages, which used technology to lower the commissions charged to traders. The launch of Individual Retirement Accounts (IRAs) and employer-funded 401(K) plans also put more people, and more money, into the stock market.

Many people blame the dot-bomb of 2000, led by technology stocks, for the fall of stock ownership. But stock ownership in various forms peaked in 2007, not 2000, at about 65%. [275] In 2018 this had fallen to 55%.

More important, the amount of stock held by various people shifted dramatically. In the 1950s, at the height of the manufacturing age, stock was broadly held by pension funds and other institutions. Entrepreneurial companies were usually small and private.

Most tech companies are very entrepreneurial, with strong leaders at the top who control most of the equity, even after the company becomes publicly traded. Bill Gates kept his stake in Microsoft high because he feared losing control of an independent board, as Steve Jobs famously had at Apple.

Founders fight this with "dual-share" listings. This began in the newspaper business, with *The New York Times*. They went public in 1967 but 90% of the voting shares are held by descendants of Adolf Ochs [276], who bought the paper in 1896. The current publisher, A.G. Sulzberger,[277] is the 6th in a hereditary line that stretches back over 120 years.

In a dual-share corporate structure, founders control most voting shares, while the shares held by other investors have more limited rights. This has become increasingly popular among tech companies, as the market has imposed no penalty for it. Google and Alibaba are just two of the many companies that use this structure. It has also moved companies in other industries, like the apparel company Under Armour, to create a dual-share structure benefitting its founder Kevin Plank, and his heirs.

These founders can't be moved out. We found out just how big a problem that can be in 2019, when WeWork failed in its effort to launch a public offering. The main venture funder, Softbank's Vision Fund, had

---

275 Statista is a site that tracks market statistics. https://www.statista.com/statistics/270034/percentage-of-us-adults-to-have-money-invested-in-the-stock-market/
276 Here is the Adolph Ochs biography on Wikipedia https://en.wikipedia.org/wiki/Adolph_Ochs
277 Here is the page on A.G. Sulzberger. I call him Sulzberger V, as we do with other hereditary leaders like Louis XVI https://en.wikipedia.org/wiki/A._G._Sulzberger

to pay over \$1 billion to get founder Adam Neumann out. But we haven't yet confronted the impact of this on successful companies. Larry Page and Sergey Brin no longer work at Google, yet they and their heirs could control it for centuries, through voting stock.

Maybe money will learn a lesson from this.

As companies fueled by Moore's Law grew, as the number of dual-share companies rose, and as individuals retreated from the stock market, the number of people gaining the primary financial benefits of Moore's Law has gone down. Wealth concentration has increased.[278] In 2021 Elon Musk and Jeff Bezos control as much wealth as 50% of their countrymen, thanks to Moore's Law, through their stakes in Tesla and Amazon.Com, respectively.

This "cult of the founder," sometimes called "the cult of the entrepreneur," has helped fuel a political backlash against tech companies. The noise made by some right-wing tech billionaires, like eBay and Facebook backer Peter Thiel and former Uber CEO Travis Kalanick, on behalf of privilege has only made the noise worse.

The risk is that anger toward the people who control technology can blossom into anger at technology itself. The problem isn't Moore's Law, but the actual law, and reform is needed.


## MOORE'S LAW OF IGNORANCE

In defending the idea of elite education for black men in the 19th century, W.E.B. DuBois coined the term "The Talented Tenth."[279] During the Jim Crow era Booker T. Washington supported trade schools and saw limits to how much black men might learn without inspiring a backlash. DuBois, then teaching in Atlanta, saw classical education building an elite that would fight for social change.

Some echoes of the Washington-DuBois debate abide in the

278 Some statistics on inequality https://inequality.org/facts/wealth-inequality/
279 DuBois' concept is often misunderstood. Here's a Wikipedia page on it. https://en.wikipedia.org/wiki/The_Talented_Tenth

technology industry's support of charter schools.

As the quality of public education declined in the late 20th century, partly due to its inability to afford the latest technology, technologists came to support taking control of education out of the hands of voters and putting it in the hands of business.

A charter is a contract, signed between a company or foundation and a public school, under which the private group will run a school and the taxpayers will fund it. The movement began just as Moore's Law began exploding in the 1980s. As this was written about 5% of children went to charter schools.

My son went to a charter school for two years and it was a much better experience than either of my kids got from the public system in Atlanta. But not all charter schools are superior to public schools. Some have political or religious agendas that contradict the need of society to discover and nurture talent.

The Bill and Melinda Gates Foundation has become a primary funder of charter school initiatives, alongside more conservative groups like the Walton Family Foundation.[280] Other supporters include Michael Dell and Facebook CEO Mark Zuckerberg.

The Gates vision of charter schools[281] is that expertise can create excellence where democracy gets bogged down. Many charter schools have very high standards, excellent technology platforms, and support from local businesses. Others are just ways in which religious groups or white parents can impose their own views on kids, using public money.

The growing backlash against charter schools for both fostering elite education (to staff future technology companies) and controlling the public purse for private purposes, [282] also has the effect of fueling a backlash against technologists who become the face of the movement.

The cost of education, which Moore's Law and the Internet can

---

280 https://www.apnews.com/92dc914dd97c487a9b9aa4b006909a8c
281 The Gates Foundation page on charter schools. https://www.gatesfoundation.org/media-center/press-releases/2003/06/investing-in-highquality-charter-schools
282 This is a good article on that controversy https://www.chalkbeat.org/posts/us/2019/07/01/a-battle-for-survival-national-alliance-public-charters/

ameliorate, has become politically charged. Liberal groups that had supporters of technology during the Obama era now demand a level playing field for all children, condemning both technology and technologists as elites.

The irony is that neither elite education nor birth guarantee anyone a place in the technology elite. Talent can be found anywhere.

It's an open question whether technologists can find enough of it, and nurture it enough, to keep growing and expanding the world of Moore's Law. It's also an open question whether enough people will find their way into technology to sustain political support for it, at the heart of the economic system

## MOORE'S LAW OF RECYCLING

The solution to the Great Depression involved creating demand through new money. Wall Street resisted this fiercely, believing only precious metals were money. But money is a medium of exchange. Money in a vault does nothing. Inflation encouraged investment and gave workers the cash needed to buy what factories were making. It created a virtuous cycle.

The solution to the present problem is similar. Wealth needs to be recycled. Money that's now passively tied in stock needs to go back into the economy, invested in things that create human capital.

The "Wealth Tax" proposed in 2019 by Elizabeth Warren is one way to do this. There are others contained in the 2021 agenda of President Joe Biden. The point is that some of the assets presently doing nothing in private hands needs to be turned toward investing in the public good, in social goods the wealthy don't have the means to create.

This understanding has created a reverse polarity in American politics, with liberals dominating the major tech sectors of San Francisco, Seattle, Boston, and New York. [283] Conservatives, meanwhile, rule where the control of land, or what's under it, still dominates the wealth-

283

creation process.

People in places I call "Techlandia" promote density, allowing people in the market to be in constant touch with one another. Density results in high demand for city services, for the shared infrastructure of transportation and police. It creates support for education, because tech workers are highly educated and want their kids to be, too. By contrast, areas I call "Trumpistan" support low tax rates on behalf of those who already have wealth and claim no need for public services because of low population density.

Liberal demands don't find opposition among most technology leaders for the same reason auto companies opposed their workers. Most technology executives recognize that they need high-quality human capital to keep growing. Thus, most support policies that contribute to the recycling of wealth into the search for new talent. They're just more moderate about it than the activists.

As we saw during the Obama Administration, technology companies support immigration, education, and initiatives to fight climate change. They support funding government, at every level, to serve their needs. This is certain to be one of the political themes of the 2020s, as government and society adapt to the needs of technology.

## MOORE ON STREAMING

Where Moore's Law of Content meets Moore's Law of Software, as we saw in Chapter 11, we need new solutions that can bring more content creators a living wage, despite the lack of a distribution cost.

This is the streaming dilemma. I find it when trying to sell, and profit from this book. Musicians find it when they try to go to market with their music. Movie and TV producers are about to learn this hard lesson as well.

Let's start this story at the beginning, too, with the small files we call print.

# STREAM THIS BOOK

While the value of the software my wife works on is constantly increasing, providing value each time the program is used, the same is not true of this book. You may read it through once, you may read it through twice. You may not even finish it.

Authors could tolerate public libraries and second-hand shops. It's increasingly difficult to make a living with Amazon, which now has a stranglehold on the market. There's not enough money in the Amazon model for agents, not enough for editors, not even enough for marketing. By driving distribution costs to nothing, Amazon squeezed money out of the book business and unemployed everyone between a writer and her market.

Kindle Unlimited has provided a partial solution. It's streaming for books. You pay $10/month and gain access to everything within the Kindle Unlimited library. You also get the chance to buy books similar to those you may have just read, often at low prices.

My family has used this service for a few years. It is constantly improving. We may spend $200 in a year this way. But some writers are also making a living, including writers who couldn't before because they didn't interest publishers in their work, or find agents. Today Kafka would write for the Kindle and may not have to work at the tax office.

Then there's journalism, the heart of my own writing enterprise.

Over 40 years ago, at Northwestern's Medill School of Journalism, I was taught that a newspaper or magazine is in the business or organizing and advocating a place, industry, or lifestyle. I was also told that a journalist is someone who works for someone buying ink by the barrel, the key part of that phrase being "works for someone." Later I was taught a third rule: always be wary of any business where the first word is submission.

The problems of book writers are now destroying magazines and newspapers. The subscription-based business model worked because of advertising. Readers paid the cost of getting the newspaper or magazine to them, not for the editorial content, which with newspapers amounted to 8% of the whole. But readers didn't know that.

Google, Facebook and (now) Amazon have taken the ad money away.

Very few papers have made the subscription model work. An effort to put together a "Kindle Unlimited" for magazines also failed. Those local newspapers that still exist are derided as "news pamphlets" by readers. Many cities, like New Orleans, no longer have a newspaper at all.

The Internet has killed the newspaper and magazine industries. I predicted this would happen 25 years ago. It doesn't help that I was right. There's still a huge problem that must be addressed if writers are going to make a living, and if readers are going to continue to get the products that writers produce.

## PAY PER PIECE

I have proposed a partial solution.

Offer per-piece or per-day access to any paper with a paywall.

Have a trusted third party, like Google or Amazon, handle the back-end through an app or browser extension. Each time a paywall is hit the app would show a price for admittance, and users would have a rolling account with the service. Publishers would not only get cash, but other data on the people reading their stuff.

In theory, readers could also get money put back into the account when they do something on behalf of the publisher or one of its advertisers. I worked on a system that worked like this 20 years ago, called Queit. The dot-com collapse killed it before it had a chance to be tried out.

But the solution would still work without this tweak.

Publishers who insist on a $100/year subscription each time someone reads the 4th story in a month are killing themselves. They need a way to capture revenue from these readers.

A pay-per-use or pay-per-day model could work. The problem is that the papers don't trust any intermediaries and lack the technical chops to do this themselves. They'd rather die than take money from the companies they think killed them.

Those companies that refuse to adapt will die.

## MOORE MUSIC, MOORE TELEVISION

The situation for musicians is even more dire than it is for writers.

The business of recording a disk and selling it for $15 has been replaced by the "streaming" model, in which I can get all the music I want for $10 per month.

This has destroyed the industry's cash flow. Well, it's destroyed the cash flow of working musicians. Record labels that hold copyrights are doing fine. Major artists, those whose names are on the recordings, can also do OK, although not as well as before.

But unless an artist owns their own copyrights, and the vast majority don't, they're out of luck. The side men, the back-up artists who make the music, and the minor artists who make the new music, don't make money from streaming, and thus don't get heard. There isn't enough money in streaming to build word of mouth.

While people producing TV shows and movies think they're doing very well today, they're about to go down the same streaming rathole.

If you get cable television, you're paying $150 per month for a constantly changing set of 50-100 programs. Most are also supported by advertising. It's a sweet deal for the programmers, and those making the programs.

But how many streaming services do you really need? Think about it. After you finish a show on Amazon Prime, you can watch anything else on the service. The same is true for Netflix, for Disney's Hulu, for any streaming service. Over the next few years, most consumers will settle on 1 or 2, perhaps 3 streaming services (if you count live sports). The amount of money going through Internet service providers to programmers won't be $150/month, but more like $30.

What happens to program creators then? The same thing that's happening to musicians now.

## MOORE BUYING TIME

One solution I've proposed is buying time rather than subscriptions.

Set a price, say $3 per hour, for a viewer's streaming time. Let them access anything they want for that price, from any provider, just as would be done with the pay per piece model I described for print content. The average cable bill today comes to $150. This model would pay for 50 hours each month of entertainment at the same price.

Isn't your entertainment time worth $3/hour? You can still sell streaming subscriptions, but this model brings more money to content providers, and gives viewers a wider list of program options.

Once you drop cable, this option is also affordable for most people. You can watch free YouTube videos, buy subscriptions to streaming services, or pay for your time. If the price looks too high, do what people do already with Pay Per View fights. Get together with friends.

In the end the problems of creators created by Moore's Law of Software are business model problems. They won't be solved by technology alone. They won't be solved by any individual content provider alone.

They can only be solved through a mix of technology, business imagination, and industry cooperation.

# Moore's Law of the Environment

This is a product of Moore's Second Law we are only now starting to reckon with. Moore's Law of the Environment is that the bill for Moore's Law is always going up and remains unpaid.

From the start, producing chips has been a dirty business. There are corrosive acids involved. Many chemicals are used once and then must be discarded.

In a competitive market, these costs, as well as the high costs of skilled labor, pushed Intel to move production offshore decades ago. Chip production, even more than oil, became a race to the bottom, as companies sought to avoid pollution costs and keep labor costs from reducing their competitiveness.

Add recycling to the bill.

It costs more money to recycle the parts in a computer than to get another computer. Computers and phones have lots of metals and other parts that can corrode in landfills. The environmental damage caused by Moore's Law, an inability to recycle, may be as great as that from Moore's Second Law.

# Moore Must Pay it Forward

There are two ways to deal with Moore's Law of the Environment.

The first would be a global treaty forcing chip companies to clean up their mess. Chip producers need to be taxed based on the cost of remediating their environmental costs. Someone must do the remediation, and they must be paid.

How can this be done?

One way would be through a deposit, pitched slightly higher than the cost of recycling, and applied to every electronic device that's sold, at the point where it leaves the factory and enters the distribution channel. Moore's Law means costs keep declining. This should not be burdensome.

The result should be the creation of new businesses whose aim is to recover the valuable metal parts in electronic devices and recycle the rest. They can be governed by the same global treaty covering chip companies.

The environmental bill for Moore's Law has gone unpaid for too long.


## Moore and Monopoly

In the world of Moore's Law, politicians constantly confuse temporary business advantage with permanent monopoly domination.

This has never been truer than in the case of the cloud.

It's true that fewer than a dozen companies -- the five American Cloud Czars and the four Chinese "Cloud Emperors" -- Alibaba, TenCent, Baidu and JD.Com -- control most of the world's cloud data centers. Most of these companies didn't exist a generation ago.

But there is no guarantee these monopolies will hold.

In 2019 any company can have a cloud. All they need to do is rack some servers in the halls of a company like Equinix or Digital Realty, which already hosts cloud servers and cloud communications. The basic software is open source.

Once a company's own resources are made cloud-ready, paying off their technology debt, they can then bring customer-facing services into their own cloud by adding more servers. Once they have enough capacity, they can build their own data centers and stop paying rent.

This is certain to happen in the next decade. The only advantage the Cloud Czars have lie in the market control they have achieved in other ways. Microsoft, through its software. Apple, through its hardware. Google, through its search services. Facebook through its social services. Amazon through its warehousing and delivery infrastructure. Even these advantages are not insurmountable.

Regulation of the Internet should still be as light as possible. Governments can't adapt to change nearly as well as individuals can, as markets can, as business can.

Using Moore's Law, the five Cloud Czars created a new communications infrastructure after billions of dollars from government failed. Those companies that were willing to take big risks to build networks of cloud data centers have reaped the rewards. Isn't that how capitalism is supposed to work? You find a better way to do something, you save customers money, you do more for less, and you earn the business. The alternative is a highly regimented system that benefits old monopolists like AT&T at the expense of industry and consumers. Do that and the only winner will be China.

In the earlier versions of this book, I focused on the problems of monopoly, subsidy, and limits on the flow of capital, as hindering the progress of Moore's Law, threatening to set it spinning backward.

**I was wrong.**

Even while writing a book about Moore's Law, I underestimated it, and the power of Internet technology.

The Internet is resilient because the network is designed to route around blockages. If data can't get from A to B, an Internet router will automatically find a path through C, D, and E.

The ability of Moore's Law to put more computing power into people's hands, every year, means a woman living in a remote African village in 2019 has access to the world's markets, and can participate in the global marketplace of ideas.

Since the 21st century began, and I began my work chronicling Moore's Law, over 1 billion people in Asia, Africa, and South America have been pulled into the global middle class. That doesn't make them rich. It means they have homes, essential services, schooling for their children and hope for the future.

In one decade, Moore's Law has turned the whole world upside down. Americans who once had absolute control over other countries because they had access to technology and those other people didn't, have lost their monopoly on the power of information.

If Moore's Law and free capital could do all this in just one decade, what makes any policymaker think that even the Cloud Czars can't be overthrown in the next decade?

## Subsidizing Moore's Law

If there is a threat to American economic and political power in the 2020s, it lies in how other countries have learned how to take advantage of Moore's Law.

In 20 years, China has gone from being an industrial country into a post-industrial one, the only serious economic rival to the United States. It has done this by accepting, even subsidizing, the process of change Moore's Law makes possible.

China's huge semiconductor factories, its assembly plants, and its support of entrepreneurs, created a synergistic system with U.S. tech companies throughout the 2010s. Designs would go through Taiwan to mainland China, they would be turned into products, and those products would be sold by U.S. companies like Apple around the world, even into China itself.

China was able to do this by refusing to respect Western ideas about labor rights, about the need to protect the environment, even about intellectual capital, ideas built up laboriously through over a century.

Once most of its people were in cities, of course, China began raising their pay, creating a consumer economy second in size only to that of the U.S. The country became more serious about the environment, becoming the largest supplier of, and market for, solar panels, pushing the cost of renewable energy below that of coal.

China also became a net exporter of intellectual property, with its own "Cloud Emperors" -- Alibaba, Tencent JD.Com, and Baidu. By 2019 Alibaba had 20% of Asia's cloud market, more than even Amazon. It was using its cloud to sell complete database-driven application suites, solutions it took America decades to evolve.

The climax of all this, in 2019, was a ruinous trade war begun by President Donald Trump. He has ginned up talk about "Red China" and Chinese intellectual property "theft," ignoring the fact that America didn't respect labor rights, the environment, or intellectual property until it was in our best interest, either.

Trade wars are unhealthy for economies and other living things. I came up with this re-working of an old anti-Vietnam war saying to describe what is happening late in 2019. Oh, and have you been to Vietnam lately? It's becoming China's China, the factory nation used when labor costs rise. America is also using Vietnam, and other Southeast Asian nations, to bypass supply chains that now go through China.

In 2019 China's "Cloud Emperors" were still worth much less than the Cloud Czars, but in 2020 China's government began moving against their power. Antitrust policies were created and enforced, not just in the name of fairness but in preventing a challenge to the regime.

## PAYING MOORE'S LAW FORWARD

The changes worked by Moore's Law come faster and faster. No lead is safe.

America's role isn't safe, either.

The rise of a religious, authoritarian, and even anti-intellectual Republican Party in this decade represents a much greater threat to American power in technology than China.

In the world created by Moore's Law, the gating factor to economic growth is no longer money, infrastructure, or even resources, the forces that powered America into the post-industrial age.

The gating factor is human capital. Trained, active, engaged minds, using the tools of Moore's Law, and creating new tools built upon them, are what drive economic growth in the 21st century.

Any policy that tries to limit an economy's access to human capital is anti-growth. The Republican Party has fully embraced a host of such policies, driven by a willful xenophobia, a fear of change, a fear of the world Moore's Law has created.

Limiting immigration means talent will land elsewhere. Cutting education, whether it's by controlling the minds of K-12 children inside limited curricula or forcing the cost of higher education beyond people's reach, limits the supply of human capital.

Hungrier countries can overcome these hurdles. You can learn about the whole world from any Internet connection. All you need is the time and mental discipline to do the work. Moore's Law means talent can now find the market from anywhere, and as the level of talent in other nations scales so, too, does the threat to America's global leadership.

The more people engaged in what Richard Florida 20 years ago called *"The Creative Class,"* and the fewer engaged in other work (or in tearing down the work of others), the more efficient we become at creating wealth. Israel is the most efficient wealth creator of our time. Countries across Asia and Africa are catching up. America is falling behind.

The promise of democracy always offers a way out, but in 2019 America is headed down a dark, anti-intellectual, and anti-technology road that can only end with the sunset of American economic and political power, a bankruptcy unlike any other the world has ever seen.

That might happen very soon.

# Chapter 13

# Moore's Law and the Future

Moore's Law accelerates change. Aging accelerates time.

I wrote the first edition of this book in 2002. It seems like yesterday. But as this edition goes to press it's 2020.

In technology, the last decade has been a Golden Age for clouds and devices, both derived from Moore's Law. So, too, in business and in politics. The refusal of cloud companies to lock-down their technology elected Donald Trump. The result has been a march toward civil war, global war, trade war, the biggest crisis since the late 1960s.

The current crisis has people forgetting the past, and ignoring the future, locked in the fierce urgency of now.

It may be the greatest mental mistake anyone can make.

Moore's Law of Health means I may live much longer than my parents did and remain active long after history should have rolled over me. At least that's true in those places where people can afford medical care. In 2021 President Joe Biden was 78 years old. My father died at 78, in 1999, and was so beaten down by decades of smoking, drinking and injury that it was a blessing.

My view is that we turned a page in 2020. The hold of the autocrats around the world is weakening, thanks to Moore's Law. It's weakening in Russia. It's weakening in China. It's weakening in Texas. We can't afford to have society run by politicians who don't understand Moore's Law, who haven't lived it, not just watched it.

Moore's Law is weakening the grip of autocracy because the gating factor for technology is human capital. The more trained minds you have, the more freedom they have, the greater their access to capital and connectivity, the more they can contribute to pushing technology forward. And technology is where economic value lies, nowhere else.

This has been true now for over a decade.

Meanwhile, Moore's Law continues marching onward, making things better and better, faster, and faster, reaching further and further afield.

In the 2010s, Moore's Law has made Africa accessible to global markets. It has made India as well as China into major economic powers. Over 1 billion people have entered the global middle class this century. They have homes, some material comforts, and they have hope. Their children will soon start contributing to the progress which Moore's Law makes possible.

But what might the next decade bring? If I make it to the end of this decade, I'll be 75, so this may be my last shot at predicting the future.

I'll try anyway.

## 2020: The End of Oil

The end of oil is in sight.

It's going to be a bumpy ride. The attack on Saudi oil facilities in September 2019, a few weeks after I wrote the preceding sentence, is just the start of things to come in what, as a young reporter in 1978 we delighted in calling "the oil patch."

When I first began writing this in 2010, I changed the headline of my personal blog at DanaBlankenhorn.Com. I wrote, "*There is no energy shortage. The sun shines, the wind blows, the tides roll, we live on a molten rock.*"

Many people thought me mad at the time, but in 2019 it's an increasingly common view. The cost of solar and wind energy, even with battery back-up for storage, has fallen below the cost of coal. It will soon fall below the cost of natural gas.

It will keep falling, thanks to materials like perovskite that double the efficiency of solar panels. Given the cost of energy-related infrastructure, the wells, pipelines, storage facilities, and refineries needed to make oil and gas useful, and the developed world has an enormous technology debt. Leaders in the developing world can bypass this debt by going straight to renewable infrastructure instead.

There are also changes in the demand side of the equation. The cheapest renewable energy is efficiency. While the size of the U.S. economy has grown enormously since 2000, energy demand is only now reaching those earlier levels, because of efficiency. Efficient appliances, efficient light systems, efficient distribution systems, efficient factories, and cities. They take less energy to do more work than ever before. This isn't changing in the world of Moore's Law. a molten rock.

Yet so many of or political systems rest on oil. Saudi Arabia, Iran, and the rest of the Middle East are nothing without oil. Vladimir Putin would be dead without oil and gas revenue. Houston would be Detroit without oil. People talk about cryptocurrency being the new money, but in 2019 the world still runs on an oil standard.

But change is coming:

1. Renewable energy is getting cheaper.

2. Climate change makes overthrowing oil urgent.

3. The change will be sudden.

The reality of renewable energy is only now starting to dawn on the oil patch. Renewable energy is cheaper, and renewable infrastructure is fault tolerant. If a city's electric grid goes out or a refinery blows up today, millions of people are impacted. Wind and solar power allow for the creation of mini and micro-grids, so failure doesn't cascade.

Thanks to Elon Musk and Tesla Inc., electric cars are a thing. They're proven in the luxury market. Every major car company now plans to introduce electric cars to the mass market.

Self-driving cars will also be a thing. They don't have to be perfect. They just must be better than you and adapt to the idiots around you. This will free millions of drivers for more valuable work.

Development patterns, built around the needs of human capital rather than resources, are reducing the need for all kinds of driving. You can get what you need online. Increasingly you can walk or bike to work. Knowledge workers can do their work from home, as I've been doing it for nearly 4 decades.

Ice caps are melting at a rate predicted for 2070. The Arctic is burning. Once the ice is gone, there's nothing to stop the kind of cataclysmic temperature rise that will kill us all right quick. It takes 80 calories of heat to melt a gram of ice. It takes 80 more calories to raise that gram of water's temperature to sterilizing, to 176 degrees Fahrenheit.

But it's not all good news. The result of oil's fall will be enormous financial and political dislocation. Saudi Arabia can't sustain its social spending. Then its military spending becomes unsustainable. Then the people revolt. All the grand cities around the Persian Gulf could become war zones. The same will happen in the American oipatch. Putin is toast.

Managing this creative destruction is going to be the major story of the next decade. It's not as simple as building new infrastructure.

The fall of oil will be as sudden, as catastrophic, indeed as violent as its rise has been. Autocrats don't take threats to power lying down. Revolutions are messy, and the winners usually find themselves surrounded by rubble. Imagine a Muslim World that can't rely on fossil fuels to keep its people quiet. Imagine a Russia that can't feed its army. If you want to see the future, look at Venezuela.

There will be knock-on impacts around the world. China is built on manufacturing, on mass production using muscles and fossil fuels. Its wealth can't be sustained unless its economy is built on human capital, on free minds. Can China continue to grow while keeping 1.3 billion minds imprisoned? What happened in Hong Kong during 2019 is just an appetizer. There is no appetite among the Chinese people for revolution, but once the economy starts to fall all bets are off.

Americans were lying awake in 2019 wondering if Donald Trump can be taken down by a free election, or whether more revolutionary means will be necessary. Yet America's path to the oil-free future may be easier than anyplace else because the technology world driven by

Moore's Law is centered here. Even Argentina, Brazil and Canada remain far more wedded to disappearing natural resources then we are. When you can make meat from grain, what happens to the cattle market?

The bottom line is this. As the house of oil falls people of the world will be rushing to the clouds, seeking salvation. But the clouds don't distribute wealth, they only create it. The whole basis of the global economy must shift, at the same time its economic underpinnings are collapsing.

The Cloud Czars, the people who know this best, have been reluctant until now to reach for political power. They fear the kind of "common carrier" regulation that eventually made AT&T stupid. They fear the kind of antitrust regulation that destroyed IBM, and nearly destroyed Microsoft. But they have no choice, because they have real enemies, supporters of those old monopolies, seeking to take them down.

They Czars have no choice but to take the poison chalice of power. There's nothing that concentrates the mind so much as knowing you're to be executed in the morning.

That's about to happen to everybody unless we start acting. But how can we even start to get out of the box fossil fuels have put us in?


## 2030: THE MACHINE INTERNET

The 2010s were the decade of clouds and devices.

But in this decade, everything has been done through human intermediaries. People did the input and the output came from people.

Even if you're talking to your computer, you're still directing it. In this way our interfaces in 2019 are no different from what they were in 1979. Fingers are replacing mice, voices are replacing keystrokes, but people are still running the machines.

That's what I think will change most in the coming decade.

It all seems frightfully late to me. I first wrote about what's now called The Internet of Things in 2002, calling it *The World of Always On*. Then again, I wrote *A Guide to Field Computing in 1993*, before the iPhone was a gleam in Steve Jobs' eye.

Maybe there is a pattern here. I get to the party frightfully early, then get bored and leave before the music starts.

The Machine Internet has been delayed by the human element. In 2019 most analysts still assume this will keep it from happening. They're pushed out the date for self-driving cars from 2019 to 2029. They think autonomous technology must be perfect to be useful.

It only needs to be better than you.

The more we can separate people from control over the machines, except in emergencies, the more powerful this technology becomes. What machines do needs to become autonomous, not just from human controllers, but from the human Internet. You keep from running people over by using the same sensor technology that waters the lawn to check whether there are kids on it.

The whole question of computer security comes down to how slow people are on the uptake. The machine Internet must refuse updates and changes except through authorized professionals, whose access is controlled and secure. Even then, the scheme of control for those changes must be limited. Use the Internet's resilience for the machine Internet, routing proper control and isolating, then automatically taking out, attempts to override it.

That's not science fiction. There are lots of computer security programs and systems doing precisely this today on the human Internet. Continue using them on the machine Internet but keep people off it the same way enterprises do it today. Develop new tools separately from production, audit changes to production so they can be tracked, pull software from production based on bad data from the field.

Then accept that there will be problems. Instead of trying to eliminate all dangers, design for mitigation, reducing the frequency and severity of problems. We do this with credit cards right now. Banks and insurers know how to manage risk. This is not rocket science.

Start on the road to automation with buses. Buses already run on designated routes. Give them fare gates and, instead of drivers, employ the equivalent of train conductors, serving the customers instead of driving the bus. It makes for a safer ride. Then adapt bus routes to where people want to go, and when, instead of using the rigid system of routing used now.

Police agencies are starting to use the tools of the machine Internet. They're linking to home security cameras so they can identify criminals and using that data to make arrests. Most crime has been falling for decades now. You can call it "big brother" all you want, but it works.

All machines, from jet engines to your refrigerator, should be able to monitor their condition and let you know before a part breaks, so maintenance can be scheduled. Factory automation has made great strides this decade but even Elon Musk knows there's further to go. No one without a college education, including extensive computer programming experience, should be inside an American factory 10 years from now.

Anything that collects data the way people can, and acts based on data, can be connected and rendered automatic. I should be the last to know about my next heart attack. Heart data should be constantly analyzed, and the ambulance should come to the location of my device without my having to call. Identifying the signs that data shows of an incipient heart attack, stroke or diabetic shock shouldn't be up to me, or my doctor, but the machine Internet. That's the real killer app.

Automating factories, automating cities, automating homes, automating all the functions of life that now require direct human intervention, is all possible using the Machine Internet. Yes, that Internet must be hardened against human intervention. That's where 5G will make its mark, machines getting the network bandwidth needed to do their thing without being told to at every step of the process.

This is especially important when I look toward the inevitable.

I'm not just talking about death, but infirmity. My longtime friend Martin Bayne warned against this decades ago, as Parkinson's gradually took him. We're all going there, although the causes will differ.

Who's going to wipe your ass when you can't? Who is going to take care of you when low-cost labor is no longer available to staff our senior centers and nursing homes? What I told Martin then will come to pass.

Machines will do it. There will still be people, but they'll be serving me, not my bodily functions. Machines will make sure I get my medication. Machines will get me to the bathroom, and machines will clean me up. Machines will produce my food, and caregivers will deliver the human contact I need to go on. People will watch me eat, and they'll talk to me. Maybe they'll be on screens. Maybe I'll move to a Senior Center because we all need to have people around us.

Sensors, motes, wireless networks, and Internets on several different levels – people, houses, floors, centers, companies, cities – these are all necessary if we're to live out our full term. By the end of the coming decade the development of these markets will be well underway.

I for one welcome our coming machine overlords.


## 2040: DNA IS A PROGRAMMING LANGUAGE

The present era is based on bringing silicon to life with software.

The next era will be about transforming the nature of life.

We've talked a lot about engineering DNA in this decade but compared with what's coming CRISPR is an Apple II with Visicalc.

It will take a generation of work, by millions of people, to turn DNA into a programming language, which makes it all sound impossible. But it took a generation of people, millions of us, to get from the Apple II and Netware to the iPhone and cloud-based Internet.

What I didn't realize in 1979 was that the future of my generation was already set. Most of my college classmates wound up in computer technology, whether as programmers, engineers, executives or (like me) just observers. None of us could see the future then. It happened gradually, as we saw opportunities and took them.

If you were in the computing field in 1979 and you stayed the course, you've probably had a pretty good life. The same is true for the worlds of biology and biochemistry today. This is where your kids are heading, whether they know it or not.

Mine know it.

My son is a biochemist, my daughter an environmentalist. They're just starting to learn their place in this new world.

My kids are also blessed with two skills that are vital in this coming age. They love learning and can explain what they're doing in English.

People love to say that English majors have no future in the new paradigm. They're more important than ever. So are other liberal arts majors. Who else is going to turn complex, raw scientific material into trillion-dollar corporations? Who else is going to explain it? Who else is going to organize it? Who else is going to teach it?

Many of our kids will be busy in the lab, or behind a desk near one, like Google engineers. They won't have time to run the companies that emerge from their work.

But Steve Jobs was not an engineer. Bill Gates was not an engineer. Once you create a business designed to do what you love, you're no longer doing that thing.

You're in business.

Now that we know where the future is coming, what will it look like?

That's unpredictable.

We can make crops more resilient to climate change, although putting more of them in high-performance greenhouses, like those the Netherlands already has operating, would be low-hanging fruit.

Things like Beyond Meat and the Impossible Burger are like Pong. Our diets are going to change, but I think the resulting food will be delicious.

There's a lot that must be done with insect DNA, both to limit the spread of disease and the creatures carrying disease. More people have died from mosquito bites than from war, and we're now in a war against nature, or at least nature as it existed before the Industrial Revolution.

There should be genetic solutions available to most human disease over the next 10 years, at least chronic conditions, at least for those whose cases aren't yet acute.

Can we solve the problem of aging? Let's see.

But it's the survival of our species that is more important than the fate of any individual, even me. We must find ways to power this planet, to re-terraform it, using the tools of biological science. It's going to take an enormous political and social will to start making progress, and these changes will inevitably cause conflict.

But there is one thing I do know.

There is work for everyone in this new world. Whether it's in finding, creating, and selling solutions to our problems, advocating for policies that allow those solutions to come into play, fighting for the international cooperation necessary to save the world, or working out the details as they pertain to cities and current farmland, there's an enormous generational lift coming for my kids and for yours.

Let me conclude with this. It's a message of hope I deliver to you, to my children, and to your children's children.

Moore's Law tells me this.

The Greatest Generation isn't the one that won World War II.

The Greatest Generation is only now starting its work.